Not Your Average Ketogen
Delicious & Healthy (Mostly) L~~~~~ ~~~ ~~~~ ~~~~~~~

****

Copyright © 2018 Christopher J. Kidawski

****

Also By Chris

The Death Of Dieting: Lose Weight, Banish Allergies, and Feed Your Body What It Needs To Thrive!

The Everspace: Utilizing the Power Of God and Neuroscience To Create Stillness Within

The Back Pain Bible: A Breakthrough Step-By-Step Self-Treatment Process To End Chronic Pain Forever

Not Your Average Paleo Diet Cookbook: 100 Delicious & Healthy (Mostly) Lectin-Free Recipes!

Not Your Average Vegan Instant Pot Cookbook: 100 Delicious & Healthy Recipes!

Not Your Average Ketogenic Diet Cookbook

100 Delicious & Healthy (Mostly) Lectin-Free Keto Recipes

Christopher J. Kidawski

Table of Contents

Table of Contents

How This Book Is Different 8

Introduction 10

Chapter 2a: Lectins 16
   Who Invited You? 16

<u>Breakfast Recipes</u> 26
   Steak & Eggs A La Resistance 26
   Poached Eggs with Tomato Sauce 28
   Baked Eggs with Cheese 30
   Frittata with Turkey Sausage 32
   Hot Cereal 34
   Spinach Omelet 36
   Bacon And Egg Explosion 38
   Onion and Cheese Quiche 40
   Sprouts and Sausage Casseroles 42
   Breakfast Ground Beef Keto Style 44
   Scrambled Eggs with Spinach and Feta.........46
   Mushroom, Cheese, and Spinach Omelet 47
   Scrambled Eggs with Mushrooms and Brie.................49

Scrambled Eggs with Avocado, Bacon, and Sour Cream
....50

Lunch Recipes 52
Steak Salad with Blue Cheese Dressing...............52
Zucchini Noodle Lasagna 54
Italian Sausage with Sautéed Peppers..................56
Keto Grass-Fed Burgers 58
Keto Irish Beef Stew 60
Grass Fed Lamb & Broccoli Cheese Soup............62
Grass Fed Steak & Roasted Eggplant Salad 64
Grass Fed Beef & Asian Noodles 66
Roasted Tomatoes, Goat Cheese and Bacon 68
Buffalo-Beef Squash 'Noodles' with Tomato Sauce 70
Creamy Broccoli Cheddar Soup 72
Cheesy Cream of Cauliflower Soup 74
Gazpacho with Manchego Crisps 76
Baked Brie with Fruit and Salad 78
Chilled Soup with Asiago Croutons 80
Roasted Veggies with Creamy Garlic Sauce 82
Cauliflower 'Mac' & Cheese 84
Cucumber Salad with Pecans, Parsley, and Garlic 86
Mind-Blowing Meatballs 88
Broccoli Beef Soup 90
Bison Patties 91

Dinner Recipes 92
Calamari Salad 92
Pasture-Raised Chicken Stew...............................94
Turkey Burgers with Sage....................................96
Pan-Fried Chicken with Mushroom Cream Sauce.......97

4

Chili Chicken Bake 99

Chicken Fry with Peanut Sauce (High Lectin Count) 101

Shrimp Fried 'Rice' 103

Pan-Fried Salmon Burgers with Garlic and Greens . 105

Pan-Fried Rainbow Trout with Lemon Butter Sauce 107

Super-Keto Shrimp 109

Pollock Dish 111

Trout & Dill Combo 113

Pan-Fried Hake with Garlic Creamed Spinach 115

Coconut and Almond Crusted Tilapia 117

Trout with Creamy Lemon Avocado Sauce 119

Baked Arctic Char with Sour Cream and Chives...... 120

Pan-Fried Arctic Char with Creamy Avocado Herb Dressing 122

Homemade Fish Stock, Unsalted, Mild Flavored....... 123

Poached Pacific Halibut with Lemon Herb Butter.... 125

Coconut Fish Curry 127

Classic Chicken Salad 129

Greek Chicken Salad 130

Salmon Salad with Rich Balsamic Dressing 131

Olive, Feta, and Sun-dried Tomato Salad 133

Creamy Spinach Soup 134

Chicken Thighs & Veggies with Cream Cheese Sriracha Dip 136

Mini Cream Cheese and Salmon 'Sandwiches' 138

Quick Taco Salad 139

Chicken Thighs With Garlic Parmesan Mashed Cauliflower 141

Broccoli Salad with Peanut Sauce 143

Smoothies 144

Strawberry Chocolate Smoothie................................. 144

Chocolate Berry Avocado Smoothie 145

Golden Coconut Smoothie.. 146

Anti-Inflammatory Spice Smoothie 147

Orange Creamsicle Smoothie 148

Chocolate Coconut Crunch Smoothie 149

Rose and Pistachio Smoothie...................................... 150

Lemon Meringue Pie Smoothie................................... 151

Pumpkin Spice Smoothie.. 152

Turtle Cheesecake Smoothie....................................... 153

Strawberry Cheesecake Smoothie 154

Coconut Cheesecake Smoothie................................... 155

Keto Chocolate Milkshake 156

Super Creamy Coconut Avocado Smoothie 157

Raspberry Macadamia Smoothie 158

Spinach, Nut Milk, and Berry Smoothie...................... 159

Veggies with Blue Cheese Dip 160

Watermelon, Mint, and Feta Salad 162

Avocado Mash Salad 164

Walnut Banana Bread... 165

Brilliant Berry Pudding Combo 167

Lime Cheesecake 169

Deviled Eggs 171

Coconut Macadamia Chia Pudding............................. 173

Stuffed Mushrooms 174

Sweet and Tangy Creamy Pork 176

Jalapeno Poppers 178

Chocolate Almond Butter Bombs................................ 181

Creamy Strawberry and Pecans 183

Chicken Noodle Soup 184

Asparagus with Wasabi Mayonnaise 186

Pumpkin Pie 188

Bonus#1: Homemade Mayonnaise 190

Note From The Author 193

How This Book Is Different

The word Ketogenic is often very misunderstood. When I hear the word uttered, most people assume it is some sort of Atkins derivative, which spirals the conversation into even more wrong assumptions. Ketogenic is not low carb, or high fat, it is a state you operate your body in, using ketones for fuel. That's all.

One of the biggest mistakes people make when going on a ketogenic diet is thinking it is a high protein diet. They eat uber amounts of chicken, turkey, lean steak, and egg whites without the accompanying fat. This stresses out their kidneys, as well as calls for insulin to turn the excess amino acids into sugar, then stores it as fat negating the whole idea behind a ketogenic diet. And this is where my book is different…

Not only is this cookbook in alignment with the principles in my nutrition book The Death of Dieting (fattier cuts of meat in the morning and afternoon, leaner cuts at night), but there are even some recipes that contain only plant protein combined with good healthy oils (gasp!) How can you have what is considered a vegan recipe in a Keto cookbook? Easy, the fat outweighs the protein and carbohydrates. And this is where most keto fans tend to burn out, sensing a ketogenic diet is not sustainable.

My recipes focus on the fat. Good fats. Healthy fats. The kind your cells thrive on. Whether it's coconut oil, lard, ghee, olive oil, or good ol' grass-fed butter. They're all in here waiting for your taste buds (and stomach) to discover!

Introduction

This book goes over 100 healthy ketogenic recipes. All the ingredients have been compiled along with the easiest method to cook them. Every recipe in this book has been explained in complete detail to ensure that you don't miss any steps.

This book will cover the following chapters:

- Ketogenic Breakfast Recipes
- Ketogenic Lunch Recipes
- Ketogenic Dinner Recipes
- Ketogenic Smoothies
- Ketogenic Snacks and Side Dishes

Great care has gone into developing this cookbook, so you can discover how to make delicious, healthy ketogenic dishes in a great variety of ways! For most people who are introduced to a ketogenic diet, the experience will be quite shocking. Increased energy, better cognition, and decreased body fat will occur and through eating more… fat! Whatever your reason is for purchasing this book, I'm excited that you did. I spent over 20 years now in the trenches as a strength and conditioning coach and had a very rude awakening when I was 28 years old. I needed a nap 3 times a day, started developing a spare tire around my midsection, and had constant brain fog. My first experience going "keto" was eating 3 scrambled eggs, and 3 pieces of bacon one morning and experiencing a most profound shift in energy and satiety. I was full for 7 hours and didn't even eat my lunch that day.

To me, food is supposed to give you energy and keep you full. I had a bad habit of always snacking, and never having the energy I wanted. People around me told me that's what happens when you get old, but I was 28! Since when was 28 considered old? I have been utilizing a ketogenic-like diet for over 10 years now and have thrived on it. Gone are the sleepy afternoons, or energy and mood swings. The gut distention and bloating have disappeared as well too. I'm a notorious note taker, and this book is a culmination of the 100 best keto meals I've had to date. While I am not a super fan of sweets or sugar, I have been known to dabble a bit here and there, hence the dessert section. For a better understanding on how to utilize sugar in your diet for fat loss and performance, please see my book *The Death of Dieting* out on the Amazon platform as well.

A quick note about your meat quality. Eating grain fed meat, or farmed fish and shellfish is just as bad as eating processed foods. In fact, I call such things processed meats! The less human interaction your food has with humans, the better, and you definitely don't want humans responsible for feeding your food. Here is a quick excerpt from my book *The Death Of Dieting* in regards to meat quality:

Beef – Beef needs to be grass-fed and grass-finished. If it does not say grass-finished on the package or 100% grass-fed, then it was finished in the slaughterhouse with a grain diet to fatten the cow up. The grains and soy being fed to the cows are not fit for human consumption and are thus fed to the cow. The grains upset the cow's stomachs because cow's stomachs are not meant to digest grains and are thus fed antacids as well. But let's not stop there when we can get more disgusting… Grain-fed beef has enough antibiotics in it to kill bacteria in a petri dish! Remember what we said in chapter 2 about how antibiotics kill healthy cells as well as infected cells? Well, the food you are eating to repair and replicate your cells now contains antibiotics that can kill your cells. Just say no to grain-fed beef!

Chicken – If you thought chicken was harmless, then think again. For a while now, chicken has become a large part of the American diet and is dubbed by many to be healthier because of its leanness. The problem is if you look at all of the verbiage on the packaging once again, it says fed an "All vegetarian diet." Chickens are insectivores, and this all-vegetarian diet consisting of soy and grains goes against what the chicken naturally evolved on. Not only that, but chicken was found in a study to contain the most phthalates, which is a synthetic compound that makes plastics softer. Researchers found that the more phthalates a pregnant woman consumed, the small her boy's penis would be. A high concentration of phthalates in men also damages the DNA in his sperm. This stuff is not only making us feel sick or lethargic, but it is also hitting us on an evolutionary level. Where we reproduce! Free-range chicken is a farce because the chickens can still be held in a crate. If the gate is open for 5 minutes a day, the producer can label their package "Free range." The only type of chicken (or eggs) you want to consume is pastured, or pasture raised. These chickens feed off the land and run around to their heart's delight doing what chickens do. Since gaining this knowledge, I have reduced my chicken consumption to about twice per month and have noticed a huge difference in the way I feel. I suggest you do the same!

Lamb – There is not too much research I can gather on the dangers of lamb meat. The primary thing we need to be aware of is that lambs also eat a grass-only diet. All lamb meat you eat as a result needs to be 100% grass-fed and grass-finished.

Pork – Same as above, pork needs to be pasture raised. The pigs need to be eating an indigenous diet and free to roam. Pigs are omnivores, so once again if a package is telling you it was fed an all-vegetarian diet, you can buy it if you want, but I suggest you use it as a Frisbee rather than for food. If you're into bacon, make sure it is uncured, which means it is sans preservatives, which eliminates the nitrates and nitrites our cardiovascular system does not like. Pork belly is an amazing source of fat, especially in the morning.

Turkey – Due to its leanness once again, I really only consume turkey at Thanksgiving. I find it to be dry and boring, but if it's one of your favorites, all you need to look for is the pasture-raised label. This ensures it isn't fed complete trash.

Duck – One of my favorites that I fell in love with in Hawai'i was duck. When cooked properly, it is the most satiating meat! Duck fat contains a great mixture of omega-3 and omega-6 fatty acids and is amazing to cook with. Make sure to look for the pasture-raised label!

Fish and Shellfish – Avoid farm-raised fish and shellfish at all costs. Not only are they fed soy, which you end up eating through eating them, but they swim around in much more polluted water. Fish filter pollutants with their gills, but shellfish, on the other hand, do not have that luxury, so you end up eating a plethora of toxins in your food. This makes eating wild caught fish and shellfish a no-brainer. With wild caught sea life, we need to be aware of mercury content. The Natural Resources Defense Council has compiled a list of fish with the least amount of mercury, to the highest, which you will want to check out in full. For now, here is a condensed version to get you started:

Least Mercury

- Anchovy
- Butterfish
- Catfish
- Clams
- Crabs
- Crawfish (try one from New Zealand!)
- Flounder

- Haddock
- Herring
- Mackerel
- Oysters
- Salmon
- Scallops
- Shrimp
- Whitefish

High Mercury (Avoid)

- Bluefish
- Grouper
- Halibut
- Marlin
- Sea bass (Chilean (I know, devastating))
- Shark
- Swordfish
- Tuna (Ahi)

I now eat fish or shellfish close to 3-4 times per night, and thoroughly enjoy doing so, especially living in South Florida where I have access to it being very fresh.

The second recommendation I need to make when following this cookbook so I can sleep soundly at night is that of lectins. There are many, many so-called healthy foods in the form of plants and vegetables that contain mini bombs that will damage your body on a cellular level, creating disease, weight gain, and abnormal cognitive function. These mini bombs are called lectins. Once again, I need to quote at length from my book:

Chapter 2a: Lectins

Who Invited You?

Forget that we are talking about grains for a second, and I want you to focus in on the anti-nutrient lectin. Lectins are so dangerous to the human digestive system that they actually deserve a chapter all to themselves. Rather than put them elsewhere, I just created a chapter within a chapter! The anti-nutrient lectin is both immunologic (attacks the immune system), and antigenic (can alter the way the immune system functions). It does this by affecting a series of proteins in the body. It has been linked to an increased risk of arthritis, and lupus (an auto-immune disease where the host suffers from fatigue, joint pain, and rashes), and it can damage the cells in our small intestine beyond repair if left unchecked. Lectins can damage our kidneys and pancreas, and has been linked to mitogenesis, or the creation of cancerous cells. Lectins are found in:

- All beans.

- Peanuts and cashews.

- Legumes.

- Cereals.

- Whole grain anything, especially pastas.

- Unripe fruits and vegetables (with the exception of unripe or green plantains, bananas, and mangoes).

- Milk and beef from cow-fed grains.

- It can be found in our chicken that is fed a soy or grain diet.

- Farmed fish-fed soy and corn.

Lectins are a silent killer, and the removal of them from our nutrition really constitutes a phase II towards achieving greater health. Much of the weight loss people see when they begin that my program is due to the removal of processed carbohydrates; yes, but it is also from the removal of lectins from their diet!

Whole wheat and whole grain products are extremely addictive. We tolerate the ill effects it produces in our body because we are addicted to them. Most people now know the drug-like effect sugar has on our body, and our health, but people have yet to correlate this fact with whole wheat and whole grain foods as well. Like sugar, whole wheat actively promotes weight gain through the lectin wheat germ agglutinin (WGA). It does this in eleven (Yes 11!) ways (15).

1. WGA behaves like insulin, which pumps sugar into fat cells not because your body is telling it to, but because WGA is telling it to.

2. It also blocks sugar from getting into the muscle cells where it is most productive and can be used for energy.

3. It interferes with the digestion of protein, and will cause it to be turned into sugar to be stored.

4. It promotes inflammation by releasing free radicals, which can thin the mucosal lining of our gut (Our small intestine is only one cell thick, but the size of a tennis court, the mucosal lining increase the depth of this barrier for protection).

5. Cross-reacts with other proteins, which creates antibodies that attack our immune system.

6. Crosses the blood-brain barrier taking with it other substances it latched on to, which will cause neurological problems for the host.

7. It kills normal, healthy cells.

8. It interferes with the replication of our DNA.

9. It has been shown to cause a hardening of the arteries.

10. It enables the entry of the flu virus by helping it pass through the mucosal lining in our small intestine.

11. Causes inflammation of the kidneys.

Because "whole grains" are so heavily promoted by the American Heart Association, and doctors alike, it is very difficult for me to convince people that anything whole grain is destroying their health. It surely was destroying mine, as I once too perceived this to be a "health" food. Lectins are referred to as sticky proteins because they bind to sugar molecules in your system, hitching a ride to cause mass destruction. Lectins that are eaten in unripe fruits, vegetables, seeds, grains, rinds, and the leaves of most plants also bind to sialic acid, which is a sugar molecule found in the gut, in the brain, between nerve endings, in joints, all of your bodily fluids, and lastly your blood vessel lining. Using this sugar as a transport, there is no area of the body these toxins can't touch!

This is the paradox we face when eating what we consider to be otherwise healthy plants and vegetables. Surely, there's nothing in a good old-fashioned green pepper that can hurt me, especially if it's organic!

Wrong. The unripe skin is booming with killer lectins chomping at the bit to get past your (laughable) single-celled wall of a gut lining. The seeds contain lectins as well, and even though red peppers are technically ripe, being in the nightshade family, they cause excessive inflammation and consumption must be limited.

The worst part is scientists believe that the rise in Autism actually correlates with the rise in grain consumption. It makes me sick to my stomach when I hear parents say they make Macaroni and Cheese for their children's dinner because it's "easy." You're right; it is easy to damage your child's brain, have inflammation run rampant in their body, and give them a leaky gut. Grains are particularly more dangerous for children because their bodies are still developing. If they get a bad signal from the food they eat that gets replicated and programmed over and over, this is how childhood obesity thrives, and diabetes becomes the new killer of people under the age of 10.

Long story short, STOP FEEDING GRAINS TO YOUR KIDS! I don't care how healthy that box of cereal promotes itself to be, the wording and advertisements are designed to sell you their product. If you don't care to stop feeding your children bread, cereal, or pasta, then don't be surprised when they are staying home sick instead of going to school. Don't be surprised by their lack of motivation to learn or their weight gain. Easy is a trickster. Your child needs traditionally cooked food like eggs, a grass-fed hamburger, grass-fed butter-drenched broccoli or mashed cauliflower. They need avocado, bacon, and steak tossed into an arugula salad, not pizza parties every weekend, sandwiched between pasta-filled weeknights because of the ease it provides feeding your child. Kill the soda and fruit juice, and give them a green smoothie or a Kombucha (Fermented tea), which provides them with living nutrients rather than phosphoric acid and caramel coloring. If you want a healthy, productive child, feed them well!

Today, more than 70% of American adults are overweight, and of those 70%, almost 38% are obese (16). This is all thanks to the heart-healthy grain veil that has been pulled over our eyes by the one-two punch of Dr. Ancel Keys, and Senator George McGovern. Are these two men evil? Did they hatch a plan to try and destroy the very country they were born in? Absolutely not. They were simply men with a job to do, trying to make a difference with what they believed was right at the time. As you can see with the second edition of this book coming a little over one year after it was first released, our understanding of nutrition changes very rapidly. My hope is that the new research travels fast. I would love to wake up one day and hear people talking about how eliminating grains in their nutrition has changed their life. I want to hear stories on NBC, CNN, and the like. I want to read about it in magazines. I'd love to hear mothers talk about how they removed grains from their child's nutrition and experienced phenomenal results. I want to hear someone acknowledge her as if to say, "Duh, we all know grains contain lectins and are not good to consume."

Unfortunately, we are just not there yet, and this book is all I can do to present the correct information to those searching for it. If you have tried many other diets in the past and nothing has seemed to work, you may want to try eliminating all lectin containing food from your nutritional arsenal. These silent killers may have been what were holding you back!

Lectin Containing Foods:

- Whole grain pasta
- Brown Rice
- Potatoes
- Milk
- Whole grain breads
- Tortillas
- Cookies
- Crackers
- Cereal
- Peas
- Sugar snap peas
- Legumes
- Green beans
- Chickpeas
- Soy
- Tofu
- Edamame
- Sprouts
- Lentils
- Quinoa
- Pumpkin seeds

- Sunflower seeds
- Chia seeds
- Peanuts
- Cashews
- Cucumbers
- Zucchini
- Squashes
- Melons
- Eggplant
- Tomatoes
- Bell peppers
- Chili peppers
- Gogi berries
- Grain fed animal meat
- Oats
- Corn/Corn products

Sorry, I'm not sorry about the long list, but your health matters to me. Before we get back to regular ol' chapter 2, as a parting gift, I'd like to share with you the diseases we are finding out lectins may be causing in the human body. This includes, but is not limited to:

- Obesity
- Cancer
- Type 2 diabetes
- Coronary heart disease
- Celiac disease
- Influenza (by destroying the mucosal lining in the small intestine)
- Irritable bowel syndrome

- Lupus
- Multiple sclerosis
- Rheumatoid arthritis
- Lymphomas
- Multiple myelomas
- Crohn's disease
- Ulcerative colitis
- Fibromyalgia
- Pretty much every autoimmune disease

Even though this list is not as daunting as the list of diseases milk provides, it still is a pretty nasty list. I don't know anyone that would be willing to tolerate a lymphoma just to have his or her daily bowl of whole grains. To me, the solution is simple; it's not what you eat that makes you sick, it's what you choose not to eat that keeps you healthy. Do not let lectins destroy your health and ultimately your happiness!

Now, it is also my responsibility to say that not all lectins are bad and should be avoided. The general lesson is, the less they are in your life, the better. Lectins from beans and certain vegetables can be neutralized by the extreme heat from the likes of a pressure cooker. If you can't do without some of these lectin containing food, buy one and use it; your insides will thank you. All lectin-containing foods are specified in each recipe I present. You can simply substitute another vegetable, use a pressure cooker, or skip that recipe altogether; it is up to you!

That's all for now! I hope you enjoy the recipes in this book and they serve you and those you love some delicious dishes, and great conversations! If you have read any of my previous books, you know I love hearing from my readers. If you would like to connect, don't hesitate to send me an email at c.kidawski@gmail.com or look me up on one of the following platforms:

Facebook: www.facebook.com/chriskidawski

Twitter: www.twitter.com/chriskidawski

Eat healthy and be well! All my best,

CK

*****Please note that all nutrition facts are estimated as no two pieces of food are alike*****

Breakfast Recipes

Steak & Eggs A La Resistance

Serves: 2
Preparation Time: 30 minutes

Ingredients:

- Four large pasture-raised eggs
- One 6 ounce beef fed ribeye
- 2 medium-sized organic yams
- Pink Himalayan Salt
- Black pepper
- One to two tablespoon of grass-fed ghee
- Avocado oil

Instructions:
Heat a large pan to medium with a generous amount of avocado oil.
Chop up the yams into hash-brown-like cubes and set them in the pan. Drizzle more avocado oil on the yams and then season with salt and pepper. Mix them around occasionally.
Put the ghee in another pan and cook the steak medium-rare seasoned the way you like it.
Take the steak out of the pan when done, and use the same pan for the eggs, cooking them sunny side up.
Chop the steak into small pieces while cooking the eggs.

Put the diced steak on top of the eggs and serve with the hashbrowns!

Nutrition Information:

Total calories: 476; Calories from fat: 135
Total fat: 15.2g; Saturated fat: 5.6g
Total carbohydrates: 9.0g; Fiber: 2.4g; Net carbohydrates: 6.6g
Protein: 2.7g

Poached Eggs with Tomato Sauce

Serves: 2
Preparation Time: 15 minutes
Total time: 45 minutes

Ingredients:

- 3 tbsp. coconut oil
- ½ onion
- 2 cloves garlic
- 3 tomatoes, peeled, de-seeded, chopped
- 6 pasture-raised eggs
- Himalayan salt and pepper

Instructions:

Heat the coconut oil in a frying pan. Add the onion and garlic and cook until soft.
Add the tomatoes and continue cooking until it forms a sauce, 15-20 minutes.
Make a few spaces in the sauce with the back of a spoon and gently add the eggs to the skillet.
Continue cooking, spooning the sauce over the eggs, until they are just set. Season with salt and pepper and serve.

Nutrition Information:

Total calories: 445; Calories from fat: 234

Total fat: 26.5g; Saturated fat: 22.5g
Total carbohydrates: 9.5g; Fiber: 2.0g; Net carbohydrates: 7.5g
Protein: 21.1g

Baked Eggs with Cheese

Serves: 2
Preparation Time: 8 minutes
Total time: 20 minutes

Ingredients:

- 2 tbsp. grass-fed butter
- 4 tbsp. grass-fed heavy cream
- 6 pasture-raised eggs
- ¼ cup asiago, grated
- ½ tsp. thyme
- Sea salt and pepper

Instructions:

Rub two small oven-safe dishes (8 oz. or so) with 1 tbsp. butter each.
Add 2 tbsp. cream to each dish. 2.
Gently crack three eggs into each bowl and top each with 2 tbsp. grated cheese, thyme, salt, and pepper.
Bake the eggs for 12-15 minutes at 325°F until the yolks are just set.

Nutrition Information:

Total calories: 479; Calories from fat: 369
Total fat: 41.2g; Saturated fat: 20.7g

Total carbohydrates: 2.9g; Fiber: 0.0g; Net carbohydrates: 2.9g
Protein: 23.5g

Frittata with Turkey Sausage

Servings: 3
Preparation Time: 10 minutes
Cooking time: 25 minutes

Ingredients:

- 2 tbsp. of coconut oil
- ½ lb. of ground turkey sausage
- ½ onion
- 2 cloves of garlic, minced
- 2 cups of small broccoli florets, steamed
- 2 oz. of goat feta
- 6 pasture-raised eggs
- 1 cup of shredded buffalo mozzarella

Instructions:

Heat the coconut oil and add the turkey sausage, onions, and garlic.
Cook until the turkey is thoroughly browned.
Add the broccoli, goat cheese, and six eggs.
Stir well and continue cooking over low heat until the mixture starts to firm up.
Sprinkle the mozzarella over the top and transfer to the broiler.
Cook for 3-4 more minutes until the eggs are firm and the cheese is bubbling.
Serve.

Nutrition Information:

Total calories: 130; Calories from fat: 81
Total fat: 8.9g; Saturated fat: 6.8g
Total carbohydrates: 10.3g; Fiber: 2.0g; Net
carbohydrates: 8.3g
Protein: 5.2g

Hot Cereal

Serves: 2
Preparation Time: 5 minutes
Total time: 10 minutes

Ingredients:

- 2 tablespoons of ground raw pecans
- 2 tablespoons of ground raw walnuts
- 1½ tablespoons of shredded coconut meat
- 1 green banana
- ⅓ cup of boiling water
- A pinch of salt to taste
- Splenda or your preferred sweetener to taste
- 2 tablespoons of grass-fed heavy cream
- A dash of cinnamon (optional)

Instructions:

Put the sliced green banana, coconut, walnuts, and pecans in a bowl, and then add salt.
Mix by stirring until all the ingredients have blended.
Add boiling water, and stir until it incorporates into the mixture.
Leave it for a minute or two and then add the sweetener and cream.

Nutrition Information:

Total calories: 554; Calories from fat: 252
Total fat: 28.2g; Saturated fat: 31.3g
Total carbohydrates: 9.6g; Fiber: 2.0g; Net
carbohydrates: 7.6g
Protein: 19.2g

Spinach Omelet

Serves: 2
Preparation Time: 4 minutes
Total time: 10 minutes

Ingredients:

- 4-5 pasture-raised eggs
- 2 tablespoons of canned coconut milk
- 1 handful of shredded spinach
- 1 plum tomato, peeled and de-seeded
- Pinch of basil
- 1 tablespoon of purple onion
- grass-fed butter for the pan
- Garlic (optional)

Instructions:

Chop the vegetables.
Beat the almond milk, egg whites, and the yolk together.
Melt butter in a small frying pan and then quickly sauté the veggies until soft.
Set the vegetables aside, respray the pan, and pour the eggs over medium-low heat.
Cook until the eggs are stiff, add the veggies on one side, fold the eggs on one side and pour the veggies over the top.
Add fruits, then serve.

Nutrition Information:

Total calories: 454; Calories from fat: 333
Total fat: 37.2g; Saturated fat: 32.3g
Total carbohydrates: 29.6g; Fiber: 14.0g; Net
carbohydrates: 15.6g
Protein: 16.2g

Bacon And Egg Explosion

Serves: 1
Preparation Time: 10 minutes
Total time: 30 minutes

Ingredients:

- 1 tablespoon of grass-fed butter
- 1 strip of peeled carrot
- 8 slices of pastured uncured bacon
- ½ cup of finely chopped celery
- ½ cup of chopped broccoli or cauliflower
- ½ large white chopped onion
- ½ cup of shredded buffalo mozzarella cheese
- 4 large pasture-raised eggs

Instructions:

Slice the bacon along the grain to get small strips.
Place the butter in a large skillet over medium heat until it melts then add the bacon and vegetables.
Sauté the vegetables and bacon in the melted butter for about 20 minutes while stirring occasionally until crisps of the bacon form on the edges and the vegetables become tender.
Let the mixture spread over the skillet uniformly, and then divide into quarter sections with trenches between two sections.
Break one egg into each trench and let them cook until the eggs are almost set.

If you prefer cooked yolks, you can just cover the skillet to allow the eggs to cook thoroughly.
Just before the eggs are set, spread the cheese at the top and let it cook a little more until all the cheese has melted.
Serve while hot.

Nutrition Information:

Total calories: 234; Calories from fat: 261
Total fat: 29.2g; Saturated fat: 21.3g
Total carbohydrates: 19.6g; Fiber: 11.0g; Net carbohydrates: 8.6g
Protein: 18.2g

Onion and Cheese Quiche

Serves: 4
Preparation Time: 15 minutes
Total time: 35 minutes

Ingredients:

- 5-6 cups of shredded goat muenster
- 1 large finely chopped white onion
- 2 tablespoons of grass-fed butter or more for greasing the pans
- 2 cups of grass-fed heavy cream
- 12 large pasture-raised eggs
- 1 tsp. of ground black pepper
- 1 tsp. of salt
- 2 tsp of dried thyme

Instructions:

Preheat your oven to 350 degrees.
Add butter in a pan over medium heat and melt, then add the vegetables and sauté until the onions turn soft and remove from heat, and cool.
Grease two medium-sized quiche pans.
Press 2 cups of the shredded cheese at the bottom of each pan.
Add a half of cooled vegetable mixture to each of the pans over the cheese evenly.
Beat 12 eggs into a large mixing bowl. Add the spices and cream, and mix with a whisk until they turn frothy.

Pour ½ of this egg mixture over each of the pans, and then distribute the vegetables and cheese over the egg mixture.

Put all the pans into the oven and let them bake for about 20 minutes until they are set.

Serve while hot, or refrigerate or freeze for preservation.

Nutrition Information:

Total calories: 450; Calories from fat: 207
Total fat: 23.2g; Saturated fat: 31.3g
Total carbohydrates: 20.6g; Fiber: 12.0g; Net carbohydrates: 8.6g
Protein: 16.2g

Sprouts and Sausage Casseroles

Serves: 2
Preparation Time: 10 minutes
Total time: 35 minutes

Ingredients:

- 3/4 cup of goat cream cheese
- 2 cups of Brussels sprouts
- Grass-fed Ghee or lard
- 1/2 cup of shredded buffalo mozzarella
- Eight to nine pasture-raised eggs
- Two to three cloves garlic, minced
- 2 links Italian sausages, sliced
- Himalayan Salt and fresh ground pepper to taste

Instructions:

Assemble entire items in one place.
Grease your slow cooker with ghee or lard.
In a bowl, garlic, stir eggs, cream cheese, salt and pepper to taste.
Combine well. Now pour over layered items.
Layer one 1/2 of the Brussels sprouts, 1/2 of the sausage, and half of the cheese within the slow cooker.
Repeat with leftover Brussels sprouts, sausage, and cheese.

You should have done all this before proceeding to the heating part.
Cook on low for 4 to 5 & half hours or may be high for 2 to 3 & 1/2 hours.
Now serve hot.

Nutrition Information:

Total calories: 385; Calories from fat: 270
Total fat: 30.1g; Saturated fat: 15.1g
Total carbohydrates: 9.0g; Fiber: 2.0g; Net carbohydrates: 7.0g
Protein: 21.4g

Breakfast Ground Beef Keto Style

Serves: 2
Preparation Time: 10 minutes
Total time: 25 minutes

Ingredients:

- Two-three leaves of kale
- 1-2 tablespoon of chili pepper
- 1 pound grass-fed 80/20 beef
- One-two tablespoon of coconut oil
- One-two tablespoon of Chinese 5 spices
- ½ cup broccoli
- 5 medium brown mushrooms
- Half of a medium Spanish onion

Instructions:

Assemble the entire ingredients in one place.
Cut the kale, onions, mushrooms, red peppers, and broccoli.
Heat up the coconut oil in a skillet over medium-high heat.
After three minutes, combine the onions, broccoli, mushrooms, and kale. Cook for additional 4 minutes and then slowly reduce the heat.
Keep on mixing the vegetables.
Now you should add 3 more minutes before putting in the ground beef with the rest of the spices.
One thing remains to be done now.

For about 12 minutes, now allow the beef to cook till it's brown. Do not forget to cover the skillet to get better results!

Nutrition Information:

Total calories: 337; Calories from fat: 297
Total fat: 33.5g; Saturated fat: 15.8g
Total carbohydrates: 12.1g; Fiber: 7.2g; Net carbohydrates: 4.9g
Protein: 4.1g

Scrambled Eggs with Spinach and Feta

Serves: 1
Preparation Time: 5 minutes
Total time: 10 minutes

Ingredients:

- 2 tbsp. of extra virgin olive oil
- 3 cups of spinach
- 3 pasture-raised eggs
- ¼ cup of crumbled goat feta

Instructions:

Heat the olive oil in a frying pan over medium-low heat and add the spinach.
Cook until wilted and bright green, 2-3 minutes.
Add the eggs and cook, stirring occasionally, until firm.
Stir in the feta and serve.

Nutrition Information:

Total calories: 591; Calories from fat: 441
Total fat: 41.2g; Saturated fat: 14.3g
Total carbohydrates: 6.5g; Fiber: 2.0g; Net carbohydrates: 4.5g
Protein: 26.8g

Mushroom, Cheese, and Spinach Omelet

Serves: 1
Preparation Time: 5 minutes
Total time: 15 minutes

Ingredients:

- 2 tbsp. of kerrygold grass-fed butter
- 1 cup of button mushrooms, sliced
- 2 cups of spinach
- 3 pasture-raised eggs, lightly beaten
- ¼ cup of buffalo mozzarella

Instructions:

Melt the butter in a skillet and add the mushrooms and spinach.
Cook for 5-6 minutes, until soft. Season with salt and pepper and remove from pan.
Add the eggs and cook, without stirring, until they are almost cooked on top.
Add the mushrooms, spinach, and cheese and fold one half of the egg over on top. Continue cooking until the cheese is melted, flipping the omelet after a few minutes.
Serve.

Nutrition Information:

Total calories: 546; Calories from fat: 180
Total fat: 20.4g; Saturated fat: 23.0g

Total carbohydrates: 6.8g; Fiber: 2.0g; Net
carbohydrates: 4.8g
Protein: 29.2g

Scrambled Eggs with Mushrooms and Brie

Serves: 1
Preparation Time: 7 minutes
Total time: 15 minutes

Ingredients:

- 2 tbsp. of kerrygold grass-fed butter
- 1 cup of sliced button mushrooms
- 3 pasture-raised eggs
- 2 oz. of goat brie, cut into small cubes

Instructions:

Heat the butter in a frying pan over medium-low heat and add the mushrooms.
Cook for 5-6 minutes, until softened.
Add the eggs and cook, stirring occasionally, until almost firm.
Add the brie and cook for 1-2 minutes more. Serve.

Nutrition Information:

Total calories: 636; Calories from fat: 216
Total fat: 24.4g; Saturated fat: 29.1g
Total carbohydrates: 4.2g; Fiber: 0.7g; Net carbohydrates: 3.5g
Protein: 32.9g

Scrambled Eggs with Avocado, Bacon, and Sour Cream

Serves: 1
Preparation Time: 4 minutes
Total time: 15 minutes

Ingredients:

- 2 tbsp. of kerrygold grass-fed butter
- 2 pasture-raised eggs, lightly beaten
- 2 oz. of uncured bacon
- ½ avocado, sliced
- 2 tbsp. of Kalona Supernatural sour cream
- fresh chives or cilantro

Instructions:

Melt the butter in a frying pan and add the eggs.
Cook over low, stirring occasionally, until the eggs are tender and firm.
Microwave bacon for 4-7 minutes, until fully cooked and crispy.
Arrange eggs, bacon, and avocado on a plate.
Top with sour cream and herbs.

Nutrition Information:

Total calories: 638; Calories from fat: 225
Total fat: 25.5g; Saturated fat: 24.5g

Total carbohydrates: 8.8g; Fiber: 4.6g; Net
carbohydrates: 4.2g
Protein: 24.1g

Lunch Recipes

Steak Salad with Blue Cheese Dressing

Serves: 1
Preparation Time: 4 minutes
Total time: 10 minutes

Ingredients:

- 3 tbsp. of homemade mayonnaise (recipe at end of book)
- 2 tbsp. of crumbled Montchevre goat blue cheese
- 2 tsp. of lemon juice
- 3 cups of mixed greens
- 8 oz. of grass-fed New York Strip or skirt steak, thinly sliced
- ½ cup of strawberries, thinly sliced (If in season)

Instructions:

Whisk together the mayo, cheese, and lemon juice. Arrange the greens, steak, and strawberries on a plate and drizzle with the dressing.

Nutrition Information:

Total calories: 582; Calories from fat: 279
Total fat: 31.1g; Saturated fat: 28.1g

Total carbohydrates: 9.6g; Fiber: 3.5g; Net
carbohydrates: 3.1g
Protein: 20.8g

Zucchini Noodle Lasagna

Serves: 6
Preparation Time: 25 minutes
Total time: 30 minutes

Ingredients:

- 4 medium zucchini, very thinly sliced lengthwise on a mandoline (Lectin containing)
- 1 tbsp. + 2 tbsp. of extra virgin olive oil
- 1 onion, finely chopped
- 3 cloves of garlic, minced
- 1½ lbs. 80/20 grass-fed ground beef
- 3 tomatoes, chopped (skin and de-seed to remove lectins)
- ½ each dried thyme, oregano, and basil
- 3 cups of shredded goat mozzarella
- 1 cup of grated goat parmesan
- Himalayan salt and pepper

Instructions:

Heat a large frying pan and add 1 tbsp. of olive oil.
Cook the zucchini slices for 2 minutes per side, until softened.
Allow to drain on paper towels, pressing gently to remove excess moisture.
Heat 2 tbsp. of olive oil in the frying pan and add the onion and garlic.
Cook until softened and fragrant, 6-7 minutes, then add the ground beef.

Brown thoroughly, then add the chopped tomato and herbs.
Cook until the tomatoes have softened and formed a sauce, about 10 minutes.
Add salt and pepper to taste.
Lay ⅓ of the zucchini slices in the bottom of a medium casserole dish.
Spread ⅓ of the ground beef mixture over it and sprinkle with 1 cup of mozzarella and ⅓ cup parmesan.
Repeat this layering three times.
Bake for 20-30 minutes at 350°F until the cheese is melted and the sauce is bubbling.

Nutrition Information:

Total calories: 645; Calories from fat: 366
Total fat: 41.1g; Saturated fat: 18.7g
Total carbohydrates: 9.8g; Fiber: 2.2g; Net carbohydrates: 7.6g
Protein: 51.9g

Italian Sausage with Sautéed Peppers

Serves: 4
Preparation Time: 12 minutes
Total time: 30 minutes

Ingredients:

- 3 tbsp. of extra virgin olive oil
- 4 sweet bell peppers – a mix of colors (contains lectins, peel skin, and de-seed)
- 1 onion
- 3 cloves of garlic
- 2 tsp. of Italian seasoning
- 2 lbs. of sweet Italian sausage, sliced

Instructions:

Heat the olive oil in a large pan and add the peppers, onion, and garlic.
Cook for 4-5 minutes, until fragrant and tender. Add the Italian seasoning and remove from pan.
Add the sausage to the pan and cook thoroughly, 10-12 minutes.
Return the peppers to the pan and mix everything together. Serve.

Nutrition Information:

Total calories: 468; Calories from fat: 261
Total fat: 29.8g; Saturated fat: 9.0g

Total carbohydrates: 12.9g; Fiber: 2.5g; Net
carbohydrates: 10.4g
Protein: 38.6g

Keto Grass-Fed Burgers

Serves: 2
Preparation Time: 10 minutes
Total time: 30 minutes

Ingredients:

- ½ lb. 80% lean ground beef
- 1 tsp. of Worcestershire sauce
- 2 slices of manchego cheese
- 4 strips of crispy uncured bacon
- 2 slices of red onion
- ½ head Bibb lettuce
- 1 avocado, sliced
- 1 tomato, sliced (skin and de-seed to remove lectins)
- 1 large dill pickle, sliced
- Mustard to taste

Instructions:

Mix the ground beef with the Worcestershire sauce and form into two patties.
Grill or pan-fry over medium until no pink remains in the center, 5-7 minutes per side.
When the burgers are almost done, lay a slice of cheese on top and allow to melt.
Divide the lettuce between two plates and set the burgers on top.

Top with red onion, avocado, tomato, bacon, pickle, and mustard.

Nutrition Information:

Total calories: 545; Calories from fat: 270
Total fat: 30.6g; Saturated fat: 14.5g
Total carbohydrates: 13.0g; Fiber: 7.4g; Net carbohydrates: 5.6g
Protein: 36.2g

Keto Irish Beef Stew

Serves: 4
Preparation Time: 30 minutes
Total time: 2 hours

Ingredients:

- 3 tbsp. of coconut oil
- 1 lb. high-fat grass-fed beef stew meat, such as chuck, cut into 1" pieces
- 1 onion, chopped
- ¼ lb. carrots, chopped
- ¼ lb. parsnips, chopped
- 4 cloves of garlic, chopped
- Handful fresh parsley
- Sea salt and pepper
- ½ tsp. of thyme
- 2 bay leaves
- 2 tsp. of Worcestershire sauce
- 1 cup of Guinness stout
- 1 qt. of beef broth

Instructions:

Heat the coconut oil in a soup pot and add the beef. Brown, then add the rest of the ingredients.
Simmer for 1½ - 2 hours until the beef is tender and the broth is thickened, adding more water as needed.

Nutrition Information:

Total calories: 496; Calories from fat: 288
Total fat: 32.0g; Saturated fat: 17.5g
Total carbohydrates: 12.9g; Fiber: 3.0g; Net
carbohydrates: 9.9g
Protein: 36.0g

Grass Fed Lamb & Broccoli Cheese Soup

Serves: 2
Preparation Time: 5 minutes
Total time: 20 minutes

Ingredients:

- 1 packet of grass fed ground lamb
- 2 cups of broccoli florets
- 2 cups of water
- 4 ounces of softened organic grass-fed cream cheese
- ½ cup of chicken broth
- ¼ cup of grass-fed heavy whipping cream
- 1 teaspoon of Himalayan salt
- Pepper to taste
- 1 cup of grass-fed Cheddar cheese

Instructions:

Pan-fry the ground lamb in coconut oil in a separate pan and season to taste.
Steam the broccoli florets until tender.
Put all the cream cheese, ½ cup of the broccoli, all the heavy cream and ½ cup of the water in a blender.
Mix until it forms a smooth mixture.
Pour this mixture into a large saucepan, and then add the rest of the broccoli, chicken broth, and water.
Mix until all the ingredients blend in together.
Bring to a simmer over medium heat.

Add the Cheddar cheese when the saucepan has heated and then mix until it melts and consolidates into the mixture.
Add pepper to taste.

Nutrition Information:

Total calories: 360; Calories from fat: 279
Total fat: 31.2g; Saturated fat: 4.7g
Total carbohydrates: 25.8g; Fiber: 15.1g; Net carbohydrates: 10.7g
Protein: 6.8g

Grass Fed Steak & Roasted Eggplant Salad

Serves: 2
Preparation Time: 20 minutes
Total time: 1 hour

Ingredients:

- 8oz. of grass-fed steak
- 1 large eggplant (contains lectins), cut into 1" pieces
- 1 medium onion, thinly sliced
- 1 red pepper, cored and chopped (skin and de-seed to remove lectins)
- 4 tbsp. extra virgin olive oil
- 3 cloves of garlic
- ½ cup of pitted green olives
- ½ tsp. of each dried thyme and oregano

Instructions:

Pan-fry the steak to your liking in grass-fed butter and season to taste.
Toss all ingredients together and roast at 400°F for 40-50 minutes, until the veggies are very soft and fragrant.

Nutrition Information:

Total calories: 410; Calories from fat: 216
Total fat: 24.2g; Saturated fat: 4.7g

Total carbohydrates: 27.8g; Fiber: 13.1g; Net
carbohydrates: 14.7g
Protein: 4.8g

Grass Fed Beef & Asian Noodles

Serves: 2
Preparation Time: 10 minutes
Total time: 35 minutes

Ingredients:

- 1 pound packet of grass-fed ground beef
- 1 packet of miracle noodles
- 1 tablespoon of natural almond butter (preferably in a glass jar)
- 1 tablespoon of coconut oil
- ½ teaspoon of dark sesame oil
- 1 tablespoon of chicken broth
- 1 drop of liquid stevia extract or liquid sucralose
- ½ teaspoon of grated ginger root
- 1 teaspoon of soy sauce
- 1 clove of garlic
- 1 scallion

Instructions:

Pan-fry the ground beef in coconut oil in a separate pan.
Spill the shirataki noodles into a sink strainer, rinse, and then drain properly.
Pan-fry for about two minutes.
Separate the noodles using kitchen shears.

When this has been achieved, put everything but the scallion into the bowl, then stir until everything mixes and forms a sauce.
Garnish with the scallion, then serve.

Nutrition Information:

Total calories: 310; Calories from fat: 270
Total fat: 30.2g; Saturated fat: 14.7g
Total carbohydrates: 26.8g; Fiber: 11.1g; Net carbohydrates: 15.7g
Protein: 4.8g

Roasted Tomatoes, Goat Cheese and Bacon

Serves: 2
Preparation Time: 10 minutes
Total time: 35 minutes

Ingredients:

- 4 slices of bacon, cooked and crumbled
- 4 oz. of goat cheese, softened
- ¼ cup of sour cream
- 1 clove garlic, minced
- 2 tbsp. of grated grass-fed parmesan or asiago
- 2 tsp. of extra virgin olive oil
- 4 large tomatoes (skin and de-seed to remove lectins)

Instructions:

Mix the first five ingredients.
Cut the tops off the tomatoes and scoop out the flesh, leaving a hollow cavity. Brush on all sides with olive oil. Divide the filling between the tomatoes and place on a baking sheet.
Bake at 400°F for 20 minutes, until the tomatoes are softened, and the filling is melty.

Nutrition Information:

Total calories: 385; Calories from fat: 270

Total fat: 30.1g; Saturated fat: 15.1g
Total carbohydrates: 9.0g; Fiber: 2.0g; Net
carbohydrates: 7.0g
Protein: 21.4g

Buffalo-Beef Squash 'Noodles' with Tomato Sauce

Serves: 4
Preparation Time: 25 minutes
Total time: 1 hour

Ingredients:

- 4 cups of squash from (approx.) 1 small spaghetti squash (contains lectins)
- 4 tbsp. of extra virgin olive oil
- 1 onion, finely diced
- 1 pound 80/20 grass-fed ground beef
- 3 tomatoes, chopped (skin and de-seed to remove lectins)
- 2 tsp. of Italian seasoning
- ½ cup of grated goat parmesan
- 2 cups of grated grass-fed Buffalo mozzarella

Instructions:

Cut the squash in half and brush with oil. Bake at 425°F for 45 minutes.
Heat the olive oil in a large skillet and add the onion and ground beef.
Cook for 10-15 minutes, until no pink remains.
Add the tomatoes and Italian seasoning, and bring to a simmer.
Cook for 10 minutes.

When the squash is done, scrape the flesh into a large bowl.

Add the sauce and parmesan and mix well to coat.

Divide between four plates and top each with ½ cup mozzarella.

Nutrition Information:

Total calories: 458; Calories from fat: 297
Total fat: 33.4g; Saturated fat: 12.7g
Total carbohydrates: 17.0g; Fiber: 3.4g; Net carbohydrates: 13.6g
Protein: 25.4g

Creamy Broccoli Cheddar Soup

Serves: 4
Preparation Time: 15 minutes
Total time: 40 minutes

Ingredients:

- 3 tbsp. of grass-fed butter
- 1 onion
- 2 cloves of garlic
- 1 head broccoli, cut into small florets
- 4 cups of chicken broth
- 2 cups of shredded grass-fed cheddar cheese
- 1 cup of grass-fed heavy cream
- Himalayan salt and pepper to taste

Instructions:

Heat the butter in a soup pot. Add the onions and garlic and cook until softened.
Add the broccoli and cook 5 minutes more, then add the broth.
Bring to a simmer and cook for 15 minutes.
Add the cream and cheese, stirring well, and bring to a simmer again before serving.

Nutrition Information:

Total calories: 554; Calories from fat: 333

Total fat: 37.2g; Saturated fat: 31.3g
Total carbohydrates: 9.6g; Fiber: 2.0g; Net
carbohydrates: 7.6g
Protein: 19.2g

Cheesy Cream of Cauliflower Soup

Serves: 4
Preparation Time: 10 minutes
Total time: 40 minutes

Ingredients:

- 4 tbsp. of grass-fed butter
- 1 onion, chopped
- 3 cloves of garlic, minced
- 1 medium head cauliflower, chopped
- 3 cups of chicken broth
- 1 cup of grass-fed heavy cream
- 1 cup of shredded buffalo mozzarella
- ½ cup of grated grass-fed asiago or parmesan

Instructions:

Melt the butter in a large soup pot. Add the onion and sauté for 4-5 minutes.
Add the garlic and cauliflower and cook 3-4 minutes more, then add the broth and simmer until tender.
Transfer to a blender and blend until smooth.
Return to pot, add cream, and bring to a simmer again.
Stir in cheeses and serve.

Nutrition Information:

Total calories: 508; Calories from fat: 207

Total fat: 23.9g; Saturated fat: 26.9g
Total carbohydrates: 14.8g; Fiber: 4.1g; Net
carbohydrates: 10.7g
Protein: 17.4g

Gazpacho with Manchego Crisps

Serves: 2
Preparation Time: 10 minutes
Total time: 25 minutes

Ingredients:

- 1 cup of manchego cheese, shredded
- ½ cucumber, peeled, seeded, and chopped (to get rid of lectins)
- 2 tomatoes, chopped, seeded, and skinned (to get rid of lectins)
- ¼ cup of extra virgin olive oil
- 1 clove of garlic
- ¼" slice red onion
- 2 tbsp. of coconut oil
- Handful fresh parsley and/or cilantro
- Pinch Himalayan salt and pepper
- ½ cup of water

Instructions:

Follow the directions for Parmesan Crisps, substituting manchego.
Meanwhile, blend the remaining ingredients until very smooth.
Serve with manchego crisps as croutons.

Nutrition Information:

Total calories: 587; Calories from fat: 324
Total fat: 36.7g; Saturated fat: 28.2g
Total carbohydrates: 7.0g; Fiber: 1.7g; Net
carbohydrates: 5.3g
Protein: 14.1g

Baked Brie with Fruit and Salad

Serves: 4
Preparation Time: 15 minutes
Total time: 45 minutes

Ingredients:

- One 8 oz. wheel mild goat brie
- 2 tbsp. of olive oil
- 1 tbsp. of balsamic vinegar
- 1 tbsp. of whole grain mustard
- Himalayan salt and pepper
- 12 oz. of arugula
- ½ cup of raw walnuts
- 1 cup of strawberries, quartered (Only in season)
- 1 apple, thinly sliced

Instructions:

Cut the top rind off the brie and place it on a small
baking pan lined with parchment paper.
Bake for 15 minutes at 350°F, until the cheese is soft and
melty.
Meanwhile, whisk together the olive oil, vinegar,
mustard, salt, and pepper and toss with the salad greens.
Divide between four plates and top with the walnuts,
strawberries, and apples.
When the brie is done, carefully transfer it to a cutting
board.

When it has cooled slightly, cut it and quickly scoop a quarter onto each plate.

Nutrition Information:

Total calories: 404; Calories from fat: 280
Total fat: 31.5g; Saturated fat: 11.7g
Total carbohydrates: 15.4g; Fiber: 4.8g; Net
carbohydrates: 10.6g
Protein: 16.8g

Chilled Soup with Asiago Croutons

Serves: 2
Preparation Time: 4 minutes
Total time: 15 minutes

Ingredients:

- 1 cup of grated asiago
- ½ apple, peeled and chopped
- 2 cups of loosely packed arugula
- 1 cucumber, peeled, seeded, and chopped
- 2 tbsp. of olive oil
- 2 tbsp. of coconut oil
- ¼" slice onion
- 1 clove of garlic
- Handful fresh parsley
- 1 cup of water
- Himalayan salt and pepper

Instructions:

Follow the directions for Parmesan Crisps using the
asiago.
Combine the remaining ingredients in a blender or food
processor and blend until smooth.
Chill, then serve with asiago croutons.

Nutrition Information:

Total calories: 493; Calories from fat: 378
Total fat: 42.2g; Saturated fat: 24.6g
Total carbohydrates: 11.0g; Fiber: 1.7g; Net
carbohydrates: 9.3g
Protein: 20.6g

Roasted Veggies with Creamy Garlic Sauce

Serves: 2
Preparation Time: 20 minutes
Total time: 1 hour

Ingredients:

- 2 cups of cauliflower florets
- 1 onion, sliced
- 2 red peppers, sliced (de-seed to remove lectins)
- ½ cup of baby carrots, sliced
- Parsley, chopped, to taste
- Himalayan salt and pepper
- 3 tbsp. of olive oil
- 2 + 1 cloves of garlic, minced
- ¼ cup grass-fed sour cream
- 1 tbsp. of coconut oil

Instructions:

Toss the veggies with the olive oil, parsley, and 2 cloves of minced garlic.
Roast at 400°F for 30 minutes, until tender and fragrant.
Meanwhile, mix the sour cream, coconut oil, and 1 clove of minced garlic (or less, to taste).
Serve the vegetables with the sour cream sauce.

Nutrition Information

Total calories: 386; Calories from fat: 315
Total fat: 35.4g; Saturated fat: 13.2g
Total carbohydrates: 22.0g; Fiber: 6.8g; Net carbohydrates: 15.2g
Protein: 4.8g

Cauliflower 'Mac' & Cheese

Serves: 2
Preparation Time: 5 minutes
Total time: 15 minutes

Ingredients:

- 4 cups of cauliflower florets, steamed
- 2 tbsp. of olive oil
- 2 tbsp. of minced onion
- 1 clove of minced garlic
- ½ cup grass-fed heavy cream
- ½ cup shredded grass-fed cheddar
- ¼ cup of grated asiago or parmesan
- 1 tsp. of Dijon mustard

Instructions:

Heat the olive oil in a small saucepan and add the onions and garlic.
Cook for 2-3 minutes, then add the cream.
Bring the mixture to a simmer, then stir in the cheddar, asiago, and mustard.
Cook over low heat until smooth and thickened.
Add salt and pepper to taste, toss with cauliflower, and serve.

Nutrition Information:

Total calories: 551; Calories from fat: 351
Total fat: 39.7g; Saturated fat: 23.7g
Total carbohydrates: 15.1g; Fiber: 5.2g; Net
carbohydrates: 9.9g
Protein: 17.3g

Cucumber Salad with Pecans, Parsley, and Garlic

Serves: 2
Preparation Time: 10 minutes
Total time: 35 minutes

Ingredients:

- Sea salt and black pepper, to taste
- 1-2 tbsp. of lemon juice, freshly squeezed
- ¼ - 1 cup of raw pecans
- One piece, large cucumber, skin scrubbed well, processed into spaghetti strands using mandolin or maybe spiralizer (Contains lectins)
- 1/4 cup, loosely packed fresh parsley, roughly chopped
- ½ - 1 tablespoon of fried garlic flakes
- ¼ - 1 tablespoon of extra virgin olive oil

How to prepare:

Assemble all the ingredients in one place.
Put all ingredients in large salad bowl. Flip well to combine. Serve immediately.

Nutrition Information:

Total calories: 439; Calories from fat: 342
Total fat: 38.4g; Saturated fat: 26.1g

Total carbohydrates: 17.6g; Fiber: 5.8g; Net
carbohydrates: 22.8g
Protein: 30.8g

Mind-Blowing Meatballs

Serves: 2
Preparation Time: 18 minutes
Total time: 45 minutes

Ingredients:

- ½ cup of almond flour
- ½ - one teaspoon of salt
- 2 cloves of garlic
- One-two tsp. of chili pepper
- One-two teaspoon of ground cumin
- One-two small white onion
- One-two teaspoon of paprika
- One-two tablespoon of grass-fed ghee or lard
- 1 large pasture-raised egg
- 1/3 average Spanish chorizo sausage
- 0.9 pound of ground pork with only 20% fat (400g/1four.one0z)

Instructions:

Assemble all items in one place.
Get the chorizo and dice it.
Peel and dice the garlic and onion.
Once you grease your pan with ghee or maybe butter, cook the onion, garlic, and chorizo for six minutes.
If the onion, chorizo, and garlic are a little crispy, turn off the heat and put them in any plate.

Now, we can proceed to the following most important step.

Prepare entire other ingredients. Blend the salt, almond flour, pepper, ground cumin, ground pork, and egg. Blend them thoroughly.

Then combine the crisped garlic, onion, and chorizo into the bowl.

After thoroughly mixing entire ingredients, make small to medium meatballs.

Using the pan where you cooked the chorizo, garlic, onions, heat it again over medium-high heat. Start cooking the meatballs for about two minutes.

Turn the meatballs once browned. Then, slowly reduce the heat to medium and continue cooking for five to ten more minutes.

Nutrition Information:

Total calories: 445; Calories from fat: 321
Total fat: 36.5g; Saturated fat: 22.5g
Total carbohydrates: 9.5g; Fiber: 2.0g; Net carbohydrates: 7.5g
Protein: 21.1g

Broccoli Beef Soup

Servings: 6
Prep Time: 10 minutes
Cooking Time: 15 minutes

Ingredients:

- 3 pints of beef broth
- 1 pound of chopped broccoli
- 1 pound of diced cooked grass-fed beef
- 1 minced garlic clove
- ½ minced onion
- 4 tablespoons soy sauce, or coconut aminos
- 4 tablespoons of grated fresh ginger

Instructions:

In a large pot, heat the broth to a simmer.
Stir in all the other ingredients.
Simmer until broccoli is tender.
Serve with mashed potatoes.

Nutrition Information:

Total calories: 396; Calories from fat: 225
Total fat: 25.7g; Saturated fat: 19.8g
Total carbohydrates: 15.9g; Fiber: 12.5g; Net
carbohydrates: 27.4g
Protein: 27.7g

Bison Patties

Servings: 4
Prep Time: 10 minutes
Cooking Time: 20 minutes

Ingredients:

- Pepper and salt to taste
- 2 minced garlic cloves
- 1 pasture-raised egg
- 1 tablespoon of chopped fresh rosemary
- 1 teaspoon of chopped fresh thyme
- 1 minced onion
- 1 pound of minced bison

Instructions:

Mix all the ingredients in a bowl, and form into patties.
Fry in a skillet over medium-high heat until cooked
through, cooking both sides.
Serve hot.

Nutrition Information:

Total calories: 496; Calories from fat: 270
Total fat: 30.7g; Saturated fat: 24.8g
Total carbohydrates: 12.9g; Fiber: 18.5g; Net
carbohydrates: 30.4g
Protein: 28.7

Dinner Recipes

Calamari Salad

Servings: 4
Prep Time: 15 minutes
Cooking Time: 50 minutes

Ingredients:

- A clove of garlic
- 125 grams of pitted olives
- A lemon
- 125 grams of cherry tomatoes (lectins)
- Himalayan salt and pepper
- A sprig of dill
- A sprig of thyme
- 35 grams of rocket
- 34 grams of capers
- 205 grams of calamari
- 2-3 tbsps. of extra virgin olive oil

Instructions:

Put about two tablespoons (40 ml) of extra virgin olive oil in a frying pan.
Crush the garlic and chop the thyme.
Combine the garlic and thyme with the oil and place the pan over medium-low heat.

Now, when the oil is properly hot, please add the awesome calamari and then cook it for approximately two minutes, turning them regularly.

Remove the calamari and put it on kitchen roll to drain the oil and cool.

In the meantime, cut the dill and combine it with the remaining tablespoon of extra virgin olive oil in a small or maybe medium bowl; then season, now add the juice from the lemon and then mix well.

Once the calamari is cool, put all the ingredients in a bowl and then sprinkle with the vinaigrette.

Toss and put in the fridge for 25 minutes before serving.

Nutrition Information:

Total calories: 547; Calories from fat: 432
Total fat: 48.7g; Saturated fat: 22.8g
Total carbohydrates: 13.9g; Fiber: 16.5g; Net carbohydrates: 29.4g
Protein: 28.7g

Pasture-Raised Chicken Stew

Servings: 4
Prep Time: 10 minutes
Cooking Time: 60 minutes

Ingredients:

- 2 boneless pasture-raised chicken breast halves, skinned and cut into cubes
- 2 sweet potatoes, peeled and chopped into cubes
- ½ cup of chicken broth
- 2 red onions, chopped
- 2 teaspoons of olive oil
- 2 cloves of garlic, minced
- 1 bunch of spinach, chopped
- Paprika, and sea salt to taste

Instructions:

Put large sauté pan (with cover) over medium heat, adding olive oil when it gets hot.
Sauté the onion and garlic until they're soft.
Add the remaining ingredients, adding the chicken broth last to make a stew-like consistency.
When the broth starts to boil, lower the heat to medium-low, cover the pan and cook until the chicken is no longer pink and the sweet potatoes are soft.

Nutrition Information:

Total calories: 696; Calories from fat: 405
Total fat: 45.7g; Saturated fat: 22.8g
Total carbohydrates: 10.9g; Fiber: 13.5g; Net
carbohydrates: 23.4g
Protein: 26.7g

Turkey Burgers with Sage

Serves: 4
Preparation Time: 17 minutes
Total time: 40 minutes

Ingredients:

- 1½ pounds of ground turkey
- ½ small onion, minced
- 1 tsp. of dried sage
- 1 pasture-raised egg
- Himalayan salt and pepper
- 2 tbsp. of grass-fed butter

Instructions:

Mix first five ingredients and form into four patties.
Heat a large skillet and add butter.
Add the burgers and cook until well browned on the
outside and no pink remains on the inside, 6-7 minutes
per side. Serve.

Nutrition Information:

Total calories: 326; Calories from fat: 189
Total fat: 21.1g; Saturated fat: 7.8g
Total carbohydrates: 1.0g; Fiber: 0.1g; Net
carbohydrates: 0.9g
Protein: 31.4g

Pan-Fried Chicken with Mushroom Cream Sauce

Serves: 4
Preparation Time: 5 minutes
Total time: 25 minutes

Ingredients:

- 2 tbsp. of olive oil
- 2 pasture-raised chicken breasts, cut into bite-size pieces
- 2 tbsp. of grass-fed butter
- 3 cups of button mushrooms, halved
- 1 small onion, finely chopped
- 2 cloves of garlic, minced
- ½ cup of grass-fed heavy cream
- ½ cup of grass-fed cream cheese
- Himalayan salt and pepper

Instructions:

Heat the olive oil in a large skillet. Add the chicken and cook until no pink remains, about 10 minutes.
Set the chicken aside and add the butter.
Cook the mushrooms, onion, and garlic until soft.
Add the cream and cream cheese and stir until it reaches a smooth sauce consistency.
Add the chicken and heat thoroughly, then season with salt and pepper and serve.

Nutrition Information:

Total calories: 523; Calories from fat: 378
Total fat: 42.1g; Saturated fat: 21.3g
Total carbohydrates: 5.8g; Fiber: 0.8g; Net
carbohydrates: 5.0g
Protein: 31.2g

Chili Chicken Bake

Serves: 4
Preparation Time: 25 minutes
Total time: 1 hour, including baking

Ingredients:

- 2 tbsp. of coconut oil
- 2 large mild green chilies, such as poblano, seeded and chopped
- 1 small onion, chopped
- 4 cloves of garlic, minced
- 2 large tomatoes, chopped, skinned, and seeded
- ½ cup of canned chipotle chilies in adobo sauce (lectins)
- Meat from 4 pasture-raised chicken thighs, cooked and chopped into bite-size pieces
- 2 cups of shredded cheddar cheese
- 1 cup of grass-fed sour cream
- 1 handful fresh cilantro, roughly chopped

Instructions:

Heat the coconut oil in a large pan. Cook the green chilies, onions, and garlic for 5 minutes, then add the tomatoes.
Cook until very soft, about ten minutes.
Turn off the heat and stir in the chicken, chipotle peppers, and half the cheese.

Pour into a small casserole pan and top with the remaining cheese.

Bake for 30 minutes at 350°F, until the cheese is melty and bubbling.

Serve with sour cream and cilantro.

Nutrition Information:

Total calories: 543; Calories from fat: 360
Total fat: 40.8g; Saturated fat: 26.0g
Total carbohydrates: 11.2g; Fiber: 2.5g; Net carbohydrates: 8.7g
Protein: 30.5g

Chicken Fry with Peanut Sauce (High Lectin Count)

Serves: 4
Preparation Time: 10 minutes
Total time: 25 minutes

Ingredients:

- Meat from 4 chicken thighs, cut into bite-size pieces
- 2 tbsp. + ¼ cup of peanut oil (lectins)
- ½ cup of peanut butter (lectins)
- 3 tbsp. of toasted sesame oil
- 2 tbsp. of soy sauce (lectins)
- 1 tbsp. of lime juice
- 1 clove of garlic, minced
- 1 tsp. of powdered ginger
- 1-2 tsp. of hot sauce, if desired (lectins)
- 2 red bell peppers, chopped (lectins)
- 2 tbsp. of toasted sesame seeds
- 4 green onions, thinly sliced

Instructions:

Heat 2 tbsp. of peanut oil in a large frying pan.
Add the chicken and cook for about 10 minutes, until no pink remains.

Meanwhile, mix the peanut butter, ¼ cup of peanut oil, sesame oil, soy sauce, lime juice, garlic, ginger, and hot sauce.

Add more water if needed to achieve a smooth consistency.

When the chicken is done, add the red pepper and cook for 1 minute more.

Divide the chicken and peppers between four plates and top with peanut sauce, toasted sesame seeds, and green onions.

Nutrition Information:

Total calories: 603; Calories from fat: 414
Total fat: 46.1g; Saturated fat: 10.1g
Total carbohydrates: 10.7g; Fiber: 3.5g; Net carbohydrates: 7.2g
Protein: 23.2g

Shrimp Fried 'Rice'

Serves: 4
Preparation Time: 10 minutes
Total time: 25 minutes

Ingredients:

- 4 tbsp. of coconut oil
- 3 cups of grated cauliflower
- 2 bell peppers, chopped (lectins)
- 6 green onions, thinly sliced
- 1 lb. of shrimp
- 4 eggs, lightly beaten
- 1 tbsp. of soy sauce
- 2 tbsp. of toasted sesame oil

Instructions:

Heat 2 tbsp. of coconut oil in a large skillet over high heat. Add shrimp and cook for 2-4 minutes until opaque and pink.
Remove from pan and set aside.
Add 2 tbsp. of coconut oil and add the cauliflower, peppers, and green onions.
Sautee for 4-5 minutes, stirring frequently.
Add the eggs and soy sauce to the pan and stir continuously until the eggs are firm.
Add the toasted sesame oil and stir, then toss with the shrimp and serve.

Nutrition Information:

Total calories: 402; Calories from fat: 243
Total fat: 27.0g; Saturated fat: 14.6g
Total carbohydrates: 8.6g; Fiber: 3.5g; Net
carbohydrates: 5.1g
Protein: 32.4g

Pan-Fried Salmon Burgers with Garlic and Greens

Serves: 4
Preparation Time: 30 minutes
Total time: 30 minutes + 1 hour to chill

Ingredients:

- 1 lb. of boneless Pacific salmon filet, skin removed
- 2 pasture-raised eggs, lightly beaten
- Pinch sea salt and pepper
- 2 tbsp. of onion minced
- ½ cup of homemade or keto-friendly mayonnaise
- 1 clove of garlic, minced
- Handful fresh cilantro, minced
- 2 tbsp. of coconut oil
- 12 oz. of greens, such as spinach, arugula, or mixed

Instructions:

Finely chop the salmon with a sharp chef's knife into ⅛" - ¼" pieces.
Mix with the egg, salt, pepper, and onion and form into four patties.
Chill for 1 hour.
Meanwhile, whisk together the mayonnaise with the garlic and cilantro.

Chill.

Heat the coconut oil in a large skillet and add the burgers.

Cook for 2-3 minutes per side, until opaque throughout.

Serve on a bed of greens topped with the garlic aïoli.

Nutrition Information:

Total calories: 523; Calories from fat: 396
Total fat: 44.0g; Saturated fat: 18.3g
Total carbohydrates: 3.4g; Fiber: 1.9g; Net carbohydrates: 1.5g
Protein: 29.9g

Pan-Fried Rainbow Trout with Lemon Butter Sauce

Serves: 2
Preparation Time: 10 minutes
Total time: 25 minutes

Ingredients:

- 1 tbsp. of coconut oil
- 10 oz. of rainbow trout filets
- 4 tbsp. of grass-fed butter
- 2 tsp. of lemon juice
- 1 tsp. of grated lemon zest
- Salt and pepper
- 3 cups of broccoli florets

Instructions:

Heat the coconut oil in a large frying pan.
Lay fish flesh side down and cook for 3-4 minutes until it starts to turn golden brown and releases easily.
Gently flip each piece and cook for another 3-4 minutes until the flesh is opaque and flakes easily.
Meanwhile, steam the broccoli in the microwave or on the stovetop until bright green and tender.
In a small pan, melt the butter. Add the lemon juice, zest, salt, and pepper.
Remove the trout filets to plates and serve with the lemon butter and broccoli.

Nutrition Information:

Total calories: 539; Calories from fat: 206
Total fat: 23.4g; Saturated fat: 21.1g
Total carbohydrates: 17.6g; Fiber: 7.8g; Net
carbohydrates: 9.8g
Protein: 36.8g

Super-Keto Shrimp

Serves: 5
Preparation Time: 25 minutes
Total time: 50 Minutes

Ingredients:

- Half to one teaspoon of ground ginger
- 1 pound shrimp, peeled & deveined
- 2 to 3 tsps. of lemon juice
- 2 cloves of garlic, minced
- One to two tbsp. of olive oil
- One to two tsp. of ground cumin
- 2 to 3 teaspoons of paprika
- 1/8 tsp. of chili powder

Instructions:

Assemble the entire items in one place.
Coat your giant, heavy skillet with nonstick cooking spray, and put it above high heat.
When it's sizzling, add the olive oil, and throw within the shrimp.
Sauté, turning usually, till they're simply barely pink throughout.
Whisk in the remaining ingredients, sauté for another minute or so, till the shrimp are pink.
Now serve.

Nutrition Information:

Total calories: 458; Calories from fat: 297
Total fat: 33.4g; Saturated fat: 12.7g
Total carbohydrates: 17.0g; Fiber: 3.4g; Net
carbohydrates: 13.6g
Protein: 25.4g

Pollock Dish

Serves: 4
Preparation Time: 20 minutes
Total time: 40 minutes

Ingredients:

- 4 to 5 teaspoons of Heinz Diminished Sugar Ketchup
- 1/2 to one teaspoon of Sriracha
- 6 Pollock filets 2 to 3 tablespoons of brown mustard
- Two to three tbsps. of ready horseradish

Instructions:

Assemble the entire items in one place.
Preheat oven to 326°F.
Coat a shallow baking dish with nonstick cooking spray, and lay your filets in it.
Mix at the same time the mustard, ketchup, horseradish, and Sriracha.
Now we can proceed to the next most important step.
Unfold this combination above the fish, coating the surface evenly.
Bake for twenty-two minutes, or maybe till the fish flakes simply, and serve.

Nutrition Information:

Total calories: 554; Calories from fat: 198
Total fat: 22.2g; Saturated fat: 31.3g
Total carbohydrates: 9.6g; Fiber: 2.0g; Net
carbohydrates: 7.6g
Protein: 19.2g

Trout & Dill Combo

Serves: 4
Preparation Time: 10 minutes
Total time: 40 minutes

Ingredients:

- Salt & ground black pepper, to savor
- Two to three tablespoons dry white wine
- 1 to 2 tbsps. snipped fresh dill weed, or 1 teaspoon dried dill weed 12 ounces trout filet
- One to two tablespoon lemon juice

Instructions:

Assemble the entire items in one place.
In a shallow, nonreactive pan with a lid, mix the wine & lemon juice.
Place over medium heat and convey to a simmer.
Whisk in the dill, and lay the trout filets pores and skin-part up within the wine lemon juice combination.
Flip the warmth entire way down to low, cover the pan and set a timer for eight minutes.
Rigorously switch the trout filets to 2 serving plates, turning pores and skin-cdge down within the process.
Pour the pan liquid over them, season frivolously with salt and pepper, and then serve.

Nutrition Information:

Total calories: 508; Calories from fat: 234
Total fat: 26.9g; Saturated fat: 26.9g
Total carbohydrates: 14.8g; Fiber: 4.1g; Net
carbohydrates: 10.7g
Protein: 17.4g

Pan-Fried Hake with Garlic Creamed Spinach

Serves: 2
Preparation Time: 8 minutes
Total time: 20 minutes

Ingredients:

- 10 oz. of hake filets
- 1 + 1 tbsp. of coconut oil
- ¼ onion, minced
- 2 cloves of garlic
- 16 oz. of spinach
- ⅓ cup of grass-fed heavy cream
- Sea salt and pepper

Instructions:

Heat 1 tbsp. of coconut oil in a large frying pan.
Add the hake, skin side down, and cook for 5-6 minutes.
Flip and cook for another 3-4 minutes until the flesh is opaque throughout.
Meanwhile, heat 1 tbsp. of coconut oil in a medium frying pan.
Add the onions and garlic and cook for 2-3 minutes.
Add the spinach and cook just until wilted.

Add the cream to the spinach and season with salt and pepper. Simmer for 2 minutes more until the cream thickens.
Serve the hake with the spinach on the side.

Nutrition Information:

Total calories: 425; Calories from fat: 260
Total fat: 29.9g; Saturated fat: 21.0g
Total carbohydrates: 10.7g; Fiber: 5.3g; Net carbohydrates: 5.4g
Protein: 32.4g

Coconut and Almond Crusted Tilapia

Serves: 2
Preparation Time: 10 minutes
Total time: 30 minutes

Ingredients:

- 10 oz. of tilapia filets
- ¼ cup of ground almonds
- ¼ cup of shredded coconut
- 2 tbsp. of coconut oil, melted
- 1 clove garlic, minced
- 1 tsp. of lime zest
- Sea salt and pepper
- 1½ cups carrots
- 2 tbsp. of slivered almonds
- 1 tbsp. of grass-fed butter

Instructions:

Lay the tilapia on a baking sheet.
Mix the ground almonds, coconut, coconut oil, garlic, lime zest, salt, and pepper together and spread evenly over the fish.
Bake for 15-20 minutes at 350°F until the tilapia is opaque and the crust is crunchy.
Meanwhile, steam the carrots on the stove top until soft. Toss with the butter and slivered almonds and serve with the tilapia.

Nutrition Information:

Total calories: 560; Calories from fat: 218
Total fat: 24.3g; Saturated fat: 23.4g
Total carbohydrates: 14.6g; Fiber: 7.3g; Net
carbohydrates: 7.3g
Protein: 36.5g

Trout with Creamy Lemon Avocado Sauce

Serves: 2
Preparation Time: 5 minutes
Total time: 20 minutes

Ingredients:

- 10 oz. of rainbow trout filets
- 1 recipe of Avocado Dressing
- 1 tsp. of lemon zest
- 2 tbsp. of grass-fed butter, melted

Instructions:

Pat the filets dry with paper towel and brush both sides with melted butter.
Broil for 4-6 minutes until fish is opaque and flakes easily.
Meanwhile, make the avocado dressing, adding 1 tsp. of lemon zest.
Serve the fish warm with the avocado sauce on the side.

Nutrition Information:
Total calories: 531; Calories from fat: 203
Total fat: 22.6g; Saturated fat: 17.7g
Total carbohydrates: 4.0g; Fiber: 2.5g; Net carbohydrates: 1.5g
Protein: 32.0g

Baked Arctic Char with Sour Cream and Chives

Serves: 2
Preparation Time: 7 minutes
Total time: 25 minutes

Ingredients:

- 10 oz. of Arctic Char filet
- 2 tbsp. of Home made mayonnaise
- ½ cup of grass-fed sour cream
- 3 tbsp. of thinly sliced chives
- 2 cups of steamed broccoli (serve on the side)

Instructions:

Lay the Arctic char skin side down on a baking sheet.
Use the back of a spoon to spread the mayonnaise over the top; this helps keep the fish moist while baking.
Bake at 400°F for 10-13 minutes, until the fish is opaque and flakes easily.
Serve fish topped with sour cream and chives and steamed broccoli on the side.

Nutrition Information:

Total calories: 452; Calories from fat: 191
Total fat: 21.3g; Saturated fat: 9.7g

Total carbohydrates: 13.7g; Fiber: 5.2g; Net carbohydrates: 8.5g
Protein: 31.2g

Pan-Fried Arctic Char with Creamy Avocado Herb Dressing

Serves: 2
Preparation Time: 5 minutes
Total time: 20 minutes

Ingredients:

- 10 oz. of Arctic char
- 2 tbsp. of coconut oil
- 1 Creamy Avocado Herb Dressing

Instructions:

Heat a large frying pan and add the coconut oil.
Place the char filets flesh side down and cook for 4 minutes, then flip and cook for 4-5 more minutes until done.
Serve with avocado dressing.

Nutrition Information:

Total calories: 480; Calories from fat: 360
Total fat: 40.0g; Saturated fat: 21.6g
Total carbohydrates: 2.9g; Fiber: 2.3g; Net carbohydrates: 0.6g
Protein: 26.8g

Homemade Fish Stock, Unsalted, Mild Flavored

Serves: 3
Preparation Time: 10 minutes
Total time: 25 minutes

Ingredients:

- One piece, large garlic head, lightly peeled but leave whole
- 3-4 pounds of fish heads and frames (as fresh as possible)
- One piece, large onion, peeled, quartered
- 1-2 tbsp. of apple cider vinegar
- One-two pieces, large celery stems and leaves, roughly chopped
- 1-2 pieces, large lemongrass, bulbs smashed, stems knotted
- 12 cups water
- 1-2 pieces, large shallots, peeled, quartered
- 4-6 pieces, large leeks, roughly shredded
- One piece, large ginger, unpeeled, crushed with flat side of the knife
- 1-2 pieces, large carrots, unpeeled, cubed
- 1-2 tablespoon, black peppercorns, freshly cracked

Instructions:

Assemble all the ingredients in one place.
Place all ingredients in a large stockpot set over high heat. Boil, uncovered.
Turn down heat to lowest setting. Secure lid. Simmer for 45 to 65 minutes.
Cool to room temperature before straining out and discarding solids.
The stock may be used immediately or, maybe, store this in single cup serve in the freezer.
Reheat and use as needed.

Nutrition Information:

Total calories: 496; Calories from fat: 249
Total fat: 27.7g; Saturated fat: 22.8g
Total carbohydrates: 10.9g; Fiber: 13.5g; Net carbohydrates: 24.4g
Protein: 23.7g

Poached Pacific Halibut with Lemon Herb Butter

Serves: 2
Preparation Time: 5 minutes
Total time: 20 minutes

Ingredients:

- 10 oz. of Pacific halibut
- 4 cloves of garlic, lightly crushed
- ½ cup of dry white wine
- 2 bay leaves
- Handful chopped fresh parsley
- 3 sprigs fresh thyme
- Water
- Grated zest of one lemon
- 4 tbsp. of grass-fed butter, softened
- Salt and pepper

Instructions:

Combine the garlic, wine, bay leaves, parsley, 3 sprigs thyme, and 3 cups water in a medium frying pan.
Bring to a simmer and add the halibut.
Add more water if necessary to cover the fish.
Cook on low heat for about 10 minutes until the fish is opaque and cooked through.
Meanwhile, mix the butter with the lemon zest and leaves from one sprig thyme.

Gently remove the fish from the poaching liquid and serve with lemon herb butter (poaching liquid can be discarded or used as soup broth).

Nutrition Information:

Total calories: 346; Calories from fat: 198
Total fat: 22.7g; Saturated fat: 14.8g
Total carbohydrates: 0.0g; Fiber: 0.0g; Net carbohydrates: 0.0g
Protein: 27.7g

Coconut Fish Curry

Serves: 2
Preparation Time: 10 minutes
Total time: 20 minutes

Ingredients:

- 1 tbsp. of coconut oil
- ½ onion, chopped
- 1 red pepper, chopped (lectins)
- 3 cloves of garlic, minced
- ½ inch ginger, minced
- 1 15 oz. can of coconut milk
- 2 tbsp. of lime juice
- 1 tbsp. of curry paste
- 8 oz. hake, in 4-5 pieces.
- Handful fresh cilantro, roughly chopped

Instructions:

Heat the coconut oil in a large pan and add the onions and red pepper.
Cook for 3 minutes or so, then add the garlic and ginger and cook for 2-3 minutes.
Stir the coconut milk, lime juice, and curry paste together and pour into the pan.
Bring to a simmer and add the hake.
Cover and cook gently for 6-9 minutes, until the fish is opaque and flakes easily.

Ladle the curry into bowls and serve with fresh cilantro.

Nutrition Information:

Total calories: 632; Calories from fat: 198
Total fat: 22.1g; Saturated fat: 45.8g
Total carbohydrates: 14.9g; Fiber: 1.8g; Net
carbohydrates: 13.1g
Protein: 29.0g

Classic Chicken Salad

Serves: 1
Preparation Time: 5 minutes
Total time: 10 minutes

Ingredients:

- 3 tbsp. of homemade mayonnaise
- 1 tsp. of mustard
- 1 tbsp. of minced onion
- Sea salt and pepper
- ½ cooked pasture-raised chicken breast, cut into bite-size pieces
- 1 stalk celery, chopped
- ¼ apple, chopped

Instructions:

Mix the mayonnaise, mustard, onion, salt, and pepper.
In a bowl, combine the chicken, celery, and apple.
Add dressing and mix well.

Nutrition Information:
Total calories: 452; Calories from fat: 306
Total fat: 34.7g; Saturated fat: 14.2g
Total carbohydrates: 8.4g; Fiber: 2.1g; Net carbohydrates: 6.3g
Protein: 27.9

Greek Chicken Salad

Serves: 1
Preparation Time: 5 minutes
Total time: 10 minutes

Ingredients:

- 2 cooked pasture-raised chicken thighs, cut into bite-size pieces
- ¼ cup of crumbled goat feta cheese
- ¼ cup of pitted green olives
- ¼ cup of cherry tomatoes, halved (lectins)
- 3 tbsp. of homemade mayonnaise
- 2 tbsp. of minced onion

Instructions:

Combine the chicken, feta, olives, and tomatoes in a bowl.
Add the mayonnaise and minced onions and mix well.

Nutrition Information:

Total calories: 533; Calories from fat: 414
Total fat: 46.8g; Saturated fat: 11.5g
Total carbohydrates: 9.2g; Fiber: 2.3g; Net carbohydrates: 6.9g
Protein: 20.6g

Salmon Salad with Rich Balsamic Dressing

Serves: 1
Preparation Time: 5 minutes
Total time: 10 minutes

Ingredients:

- 2 tbsp. of homemade mayonnaise
- 1 tsp. of Dijon or whole grain mustard
- 2 tsp. of balsamic vinegar
- Salt and pepper to taste
- 3 cups of spinach mix or baby kale
- 3 oz. of cooked or smoked salmon, in bite-size pieces
- ¼ cup of chopped raw walnuts

Instructions:

Whisk together the mayonnaise, mustard, vinegar, salt, and pepper.
Put the greens on a plate and top with the salmon and walnuts.
Pour the dressing over and serve.

Nutrition Information:

Total calories: 597; Calories from fat: 288
Total fat: 32.0g; Saturated fat: 7.3g

Total carbohydrates: 10.2g; Fiber: 4.1g; Net
carbohydrates: 6.1g
Protein: 26.3g

Olive, Feta, and Sun-dried Tomato Salad

Serves: 1
Preparation Time: 6 minutes
Total time: 10 minutes

Ingredients:

- ½ cup of green olives
- ¼ cup of crumbled goat feta
- ¼ cup of sun-dried tomatoes in oil, chopped (Lectins)
- ½ cucumber, peeled, seeded, and chopped
- 1 tbsp. of olive oil
- Pinch-dried thyme and oregano, optional

Instructions:

Toss all ingredients together.
Serve right away or chill.

Nutrition Information:

Total calories: 375; Calories from fat: 162
Total fat: 18.2g; Saturated fat: 9.1g
Total carbohydrates: 13.1g; Fiber: 4.4g; Net carbohydrates: 8.7g
Protein: 8.1g

Creamy Spinach Soup

Serves: 4
Preparation Time: 8 minutes
Total time: 25 minutes

Ingredients:

- 4 tbsp. of olive oil
- 1 small onion, chopped
- 2 cloves of garlic, minced
- 1½ lbs. of spinach
- 1 cup of shredded Buffalo mozzarella cheese
- 1 cup of grass-fed heavy cream
- 3 cups of chicken broth
- Pinch nutmeg
- Sea salt and pepper
- 6 pasture-raised hardboiled eggs, chopped

Instructions:

Heat the olive oil in a soup pot.
Add the onion and garlic, then cook until softened and fragrant.
Add the spinach and cook until bright green and wilted, 2-3 minutes.
Transfer to a food processor and add 1 cup of broth.
Pulse a few times until the mixture is creamy with a few chunks, or puree longer for a very smooth soup.
Return the soup to the pot and add the rest of the broth.

Bring to a simmer and add the cream and the mozzarella.
Cook just until the cheese has melted.
Divide between bowls and serve with chopped
hardboiled egg.

Nutrition Information:

Total calories: 517; Calories from fat: 153
Total fat: 17.0g; Saturated fat: 20.7g
Total carbohydrates: 14.6g; Fiber: 5.2g; Net
carbohydrates: 9.4g
Protein: 24.6g

Chicken Thighs & Veggies with Cream Cheese Sriracha Dip

Serves: 1
Preparation time: 5 minutes
Total time: 21 minutes

Ingredients:

- 4 pasture-raised chicken thighs
- 2 oz. of goat cream cheese, softened
- 3 tbsp. of grass-fed sour cream
- 1 tsp. of Sriracha sauce
- 2 tsp. of coconut oil
- 1 green onion, thinly sliced
- 3 stalks celery, cut into 4-inch pieces
- ½ cup of baby carrots

Instructions:

Season the chicken thighs and bake for 16 minutes at 425 degrees
Mix the cream cheese, sour cream, Sriracha sauce, coconut oil, and green onion.
Serve, or make ahead for a quick and easy lunch.

Nutrition Information:

Total calories: 384; Calories from fat: 270
Total fat: 30.5g; Saturated fat: 24.1g

Total carbohydrates: 14.9g; Fiber: 4.4g; Net carbohydrates: 10.5g
Protein: 5.1g

Mini Cream Cheese and Salmon 'Sandwiches'

Serves: 1
Preparation Time: 5 minutes
Total time: 10 minutes

Ingredients:

- ½ medium cucumber, peeled, seeded, sliced
- 2 oz. of goat cream cheese
- 3 oz. of smoked or cured salmon

Instructions:

Top each slice of cucumber with a bit of cream cheese and salmon.
Eat as a quick lunch or serve as appetizers.

Nutrition Information:

Total calories: 313; Calories from fat: 297
Total fat: 33.0g; Saturated fat: 11.6g
Total carbohydrates: 7.7g; Fiber: 0.8g; Net carbohydrates: 6.9g
Protein: 19.8g

Quick Taco Salad

Serves: 1
Preparation Time: 5 minutes
Total time: 20 minutes

Ingredients:

- ¼ head lettuce, roughly chopped
- 1 lb. of grass-fed ground beef, browned, or 1 leftover hamburger, crumbled
- ¼ cup shredded grass-fed cheddar cheese
- ½ tomato, chopped, skinned, seeded
- 1 sliced onion, minced
- 2 tbsp. of black olives
- 2 tbsp. of goat sour cream

Instructions:

Put the lettuce in a bowl (or a separate Tupperware container if you are packing this for later).
Toss together the ground beef, cheese, tomato, onion, and olives.
When ready to eat, put all the toppings on the lettuce and drizzle everything with sour cream.

Nutrition Information:

Total calories: 424; Calories from fat: 263
Total fat: 29.7g; Saturated fat: 14.1g

Total carbohydrates: 10.5g; Fiber: 4.6g; Net carbohydrates: 5.9g
Protein: 30.3g

Chicken Thighs With Garlic Parmesan Mashed Cauliflower

Serves: 2
Preparation Time: 8 minutes
Total time: 20 minutes

Ingredients:

- 4 pasture-raised chicken thighs
- 1 head cauliflower (6-7")
- 4 tbsp. of grass-fed butter
- ½ cup of grass-fed sour cream
- ¼ cup of grated grass-fed parmesan cheese
- 1 clove of garlic, minced
- Sea salt and pepper

Instructions:

Season and bake the chicken thighs at 425°F for 16 minutes
Cut the cauliflower into large chunks.
Boil or steam until tender.
Transfer to a food processor and add the butter, sour cream, garlic, cheese, salt, and pepper to taste.
Process until smooth and serve.

Nutrition Information:

Total calories: 470; Calories from fat: 334

Total fat: 38.0g; Saturated fat: 23.2g
Total carbohydrates: 24.8g; Fiber: 10.6g; Net
carbohydrates: 14.2g
Protein: 14.6g

Broccoli Salad with Peanut Sauce

Serves: 1
Preparation Time: 5 minutes
Total time: 15 minutes

Ingredients:

- 2 cups of broccoli florets
- 1 tbsp. of coconut oil
- ½ recipe of peanut sauce (lectins)
- 1 tsp. of toasted sesame seeds
- 1 green onion, thinly sliced

Instructions:

Sauté the broccoli florets for 4-6 minutes until tender and bright green.
Toss with the peanut sauce and sprinkle with sesame seeds and green onion.
Serve right away or pack as a quick lunch.

Nutrition Information:

Total calories: 656; Calories from fat: 403
Total fat: 47.3g; Saturated fat: 23.6g
Total carbohydrate: 30.3g; Fiber: 13.0g; Net carbohydrates: 17.3g
Protein: 16.5g

Smoothies

Strawberry Chocolate Smoothie

Serves: 1
Total time: 5 minutes

Ingredients:

- 1 tbsp. of cocoa powder
- ½ cup of strawberries (In Season)
- 1 tbsp. of coconut or coconut oil
- ¼ cup of grass-fed heavy cream
- 2 tbsp. of low-carb chocolate protein powder
- Water

Instructions:

Blend all ingredients until smooth.

Nutrition Information:

Total calories: 423; Calories from fat: 322
Total fat: 36.9g; Saturated fat: 25.9g
Total carbohydrates: 16.5g; Fiber: 4.1g; Net
carbohydrates: 12.4g
Protein: 14.0g

Chocolate Berry Avocado Smoothie

Serves: 1
Total time: 5 minutes

Ingredients:

• 1 tbsp. of cocoa powder
• ½ cup of berries (In Season)
• 1 avocado
• ¼ cup of grass-fed heavy cream
• 2 tbsp. of low-carb chocolate protein powder
• water

Instructions:

Blend all ingredients until smooth.

Nutrition Information:

Total calories: 533; Calories from fat: 381
Total fat: 44.4g; Saturated fat: 17.1g
Total carbohydrates: 28.2g; Fiber: 13.4g; Net
carbohydrates: 14.8g
Protein: 16.7g

Golden Coconut Smoothie

Serves: 1
Total time: 5 minutes

Ingredients:

- ⅓ cup of coconut cream
- 2 tbsp. of low-carb plain or vanilla protein powder
- 1 tbsp. of XCT oil (from bulletproof.com)
- ½ tsp. of turmeric
- Water

Instructions:

Blend all ingredients until smooth.

Nutrition Information:

Total calories: 511; Calories from fat: 380
Total fat: 45.4g; Saturated fat: 38.7g
Total carbohydrates: 9.3g; Fiber: 5.2g; Net
carbohydrates: 4.1g
Protein: 26.7g

Anti-Inflammatory Spice Smoothie

Serves: 1
Total time: 5 minutes

Ingredients:

•1 avocado
•2 tbsp. of low-carb plain or vanilla protein powder
•½ cup of blueberries
•1 tbsp. of coconut oil
•1 tbsp. of ghee oil
•¼ tsp. of each turmeric, ginger, and cinnamon
•Water

Instructions:

Blend all ingredients until smooth.

Nutrition Information:

Total calories: 601; Calories from fat: 422
Total fat: 49.7g; Saturated fat: 18.3g
Total carbohydrates: 24.5g; Fiber: 12.6g; Net
carbohydrates: 11.9g
Protein: 25.8g

Orange Creamsicle Smoothie

Serves: 1
Total time: 15 minutes
Ingredients

- ½ avocado
- ¼ cup of grass-fed heavy cream
- 2 tbsp. of low-carb vanilla or orange cream protein powder
- ¼ - ½ tsp. of orange zest, minced
- 1 tbsp. of XCT oil
- Water

Instructions:

Blend all ingredients until smooth.

Nutrition Information:

Total calories: 531; Calories from fat: 407
Total fat: 47.4g; Saturated fat: 29.3g
Total carbohydrates: 9.6g; Fiber: 6.2g; Net carbohydrates: 3.4g
Protein: 25.1g

Chocolate Coconut Crunch Smoothie

Serves: 1
Total time: 5 minutes

Ingredients:

• 1 avocado
• 2 tbsp. of low-carb chocolate protein powder
• 1 tbsp. of XCT oil
• Water
• 2 tbsp. of chopped almonds
• 2 tbsp. of unsweetened coconut flakes

Instructions:

Blend the avocado, protein powder, XCT oil, and water until smooth.
Stir in the almonds and coconut flakes and serve.

Nutrition Information:

Total calories: 633; Calories from fat: 447
Total fat: 53.3g; Saturated fat: 24.9g
Total carbohydrates: 23.2g; Fiber: 16.3g; Net carbohydrates: 6.9g
Protein: 31.0g

Rose and Pistachio Smoothie

Serves: 1
Total time: 5 minutes

Ingredients:

•⅓ cup of coconut cream
•2 tbsp. of low-carb plain or vanilla protein powder
•1 tbsp. of XCT oil
•3 tbsp. of chopped pistachios
•1-2 tsp. culinary rosewater
•Water

Instructions:

Blend all ingredients until smooth.

Nutrition Information:

Total calories: 554; Calories from fat: 396
Total fat: 47.2g; Saturated fat: 34.0g
Total carbohydrates: 13.3g; Fiber: 5.5g; Net
carbohydrates: 7.8g
Protein: 30.1g

Lemon Meringue Pie Smoothie

Serves: 1
Total time: 15 minutes

Ingredients:

• ¼ cup of coconut cream
• ¼ - ½ tsp. of lemon zest, minced
• 2 tsp. of lemon juice
• 1 tbsp. of XCT oil
• Water
• ¼ cup of plain homemade whipped cream
• 2 tbsp. of crushed raw pecans

Instructions:

Blend first five ingredients until smooth.
Top with whipped cream and pecans.

Nutrition Information:

Total calories: 519; Calories from fat: 456
Total fat: 53.8g; Saturated fat: 40.9g
Total carbohydrates: 11.0g; Fiber: 1.9g; Net
carbohydrates: 9.1g
Protein: 5.4g

Pumpkin Spice Smoothie

Serves: 1
Total time: 5 minutes

Ingredients:

•¼ cup of organic pumpkin puree (In season)
•2 tbsp. of low-carb vanilla protein powder
•2 tbsp. of XCT oil
•¼ cup of raw pecans
•½ tsp. of cinnamon and ginger + pinch cloves or allspice
•Water

Instructions:

Blend all ingredients until smooth.

Nutrition Information:

Total calories: 522; Calories from fat: 243
Total fat: 42.8g; Saturated fat: 29.9g
Total carbohydrates: 15.6g; Fiber: 6.5g; Net carbohydrates: 9.1g
Protein: 29.6g

Turtle Cheesecake Smoothie

Serves: 1
Total time: 5 minutes

Ingredients:

- 2 oz. of grass-fed cream cheese
- 1 tbsp. of XCT oil
- 1 tbsp. of low-carb vanilla protein powder
- 1 tbsp. of sugar-free caramel syrup
- Water
- 3 tbsp. of chopped raw pecans
- 1 tbsp. of sugar-free chocolate syrup

Instructions:

Blend the first five ingredients until smooth.
Pour into a glass and top with sugar-free chocolate syrup and pecans.

Nutrition Information:

Total calories: 498; Calories from fat: 419
Total fat: 49.1g; Saturated fat: 26.2g
Total carbohydrates: 5.8g; Fiber: 2.5g; Net carbohydrates: 3.3g
Protein: 12.8g

Strawberry Cheesecake Smoothie

Serves: 1
Total time: 5 minutes

Ingredients:

•2 oz. of cream cheese
•1 tbsp. of XCT oil
•2 tbsp. of low-carb vanilla protein powder
•½ cup of strawberries, halved (In season)
•Water

Instructions:

Blend all ingredients until smooth.

Nutrition Information:

Total calories: 514; Calories from fat: 411
Total fat: 48.0g; Saturated fat: 38.9g
Total carbohydrates: 9.5g; Fiber: 2.6g; Net
carbohydrates: 6.9g
Protein: 18.7g

Coconut Cheesecake Smoothie

Serves: 1
Total time: 5 minutes

Ingredients:

•2 oz. of grass-fed cream cheese
•¼ cup of coconut cream
•2 tbsp. of low-carb vanilla protein powder
•3 tbsp. of unsweetened toasted coconut flakes
•Water

Instructions:

Blend all ingredients until smooth.

Nutrition Information:

Total calories: 544; Calories from fat: 424
Total fat: 49.6g; Saturated fat: 37.3g
Total carbohydrates: 10.9g; Fiber: 4.6g; Net
carbohydrates: 6.3g
Protein: 21.4g

Keto Chocolate Milkshake

Serves: 1
Total time: 5 minutes

Ingredients:

- 1 avocado
- ¼ cup of grass-fed heavy cream
- 1 tbsp. of XCT oil
- 1 tbsp. of cocoa powder
- 2 tbsp. of low-carb chocolate protein powder
- ½ cup of water
- 3 ice cubes

Instructions:

Blend all ingredients until smooth, adding more water as needed.

Nutrition Information:

Total calories: 624; Calories from fat: 498
Total fat: 58.36g; Saturated fat: 31.1g
Total carbohydrates: 17.8g; Fiber: 11.8g; Net carbohydrates: 6.0g
Protein: 19.7g

Super Creamy Coconut Avocado Smoothie

Serves: 1
Total time: 5 minutes

Ingredients:

•1 avocado
•⅓ cup of coconut cream
•2 tbsp. of low-carb vanilla protein powder
•Water

Instructions:

Blend all ingredients until smooth.

Nutrition Information:

Total calories: 551; Calories from fat: 411
Total fat: 49.0g; Saturated fat: 27.3g
Total carbohydrates: 18.4g; Fiber: 12.0g; Net
carbohydrates: 6.4g
Protein: 20.5g

Raspberry Macadamia Smoothie

Serves: 1
Total time: 5 minutes

Ingredients:

• ½ cup of raspberries (In season)
• ¼ cup of grass-fed heavy cream
• 2 tbsp. of Macadamia nuts
• 1 tbsp. of XCT oil
• 2 tbsp. of low-carb vanilla protein powder
• Water

Instructions:

Blend all ingredients until smooth.

Nutrition Information:

Total calories: 535; Calories from fat: 425
Total fat: 49.6g; Saturated fat: 29.8g
Total carbohydrates: 12.5g; Fiber: 6.4g; Net
carbohydrates: 6.1g
Protein: 18.2g

Spinach, Nut Milk, and Berry Smoothie

Serves: 2
Total time: 12 minutes

Ingredients:

- 1 green banana
- 3 cups of nut milk of choice
- Ice cubes to taste
- 1 to 2 tbsp. of lemon zest
- One small orange, peeled
- One & 1/2 cups of loosely packed spinach
- Two cups of fresh mixed berries (In Season)
- One to two tbsp of hemp seeds, optional

Preparation:

First, put all items in a blender.
Then mix until smoothie consistency is reached.
Now, pour over ice, and then you can serve.

Nutrition Information:

Total calories: 505; Calories from fat: 383
Total fat: 42.6g; Saturated fat: 25.8g
Total carbohydrates: 12.5g; Fiber: 16.4g; Net
carbohydrates: 28.1g
Protein: 20.2g

Snacks and Side Dishes

Veggies with Blue Cheese Dip

Serves: 1
Preparation Time: 6 minutes
Total time: 10 minutes

Ingredients:

- ¼ cup of crumbled goat blue cheese
- 3 tbsp. of homemade mayonnaise
- 2 tsp. of coconut oil
- 1 tsp. of lemon juice
- Sea salt and pepper to taste
- 2 stalks of celery
- 1 cup of baby carrots

Instructions:

Mix together the first five ingredients until smooth. Serve with veggies.

Nutrition Information:

Total calories: 555; Calories from fat: 261
Total fat: 29.9g; Saturated fat: 28.0g
Total carbohydrates: 21.4g; Fiber: 7.3g; Net
carbohydrates: 14.1g
Protein: 10.7g

Watermelon, Mint, and Feta Salad

Serves: 1
Preparation Time: 4 minutes
Total time: 10 minutes

Ingredients:

- 1 cup of watermelon, de-seeded, cut into bite-size cubes
- 1 medium cucumber, peeled, seeded, and chopped
- 4 oz. of feta cheese, crumbled
- ⅓ cup of walnuts
- 1 handful fresh mint leaves, chopped

Instructions:

Gently mix all the ingredients together.
Chill for 2 hours before serving.

Nutrition Information:

Total calories: 459; Calories from fat: 153
Total fat: 17.3g; Saturated fat: 14.4g
Total carbohydrates: 18.2g; Fiber: 3.1g; Net carbohydrates: 15.1g
Protein: 17.7g

Honeyed Walnuts

Serves: 1 to 2
Preparation Time: 10 minutes
Total time: 20 minutes

Ingredients:

- Dash sea salt
- 1/2 - 1 teaspoon raw, unprocessed Honey
- Approximately about 1/4 to 1/2 cup or so, loosely packed shelled walnuts, lightly toasted in a dry pan until aromatic and brown on all sides, cool slightly before seasoning

Instructions:

Assemble all the ingredients in one place.
Put all ingredients in small bowl.
One thing remains to be done now.
Flip well to mix.

Nutrition Information:

Total calories: 396; Calories from fat: 216
Total fat: 24.7g; Saturated fat: 12.8g
Total carbohydrates: 0.9g; Fiber: 0.5g; Net carbohydrates: 1.4g
Protein: 27.7g

Avocado Mash Salad

Serves: 4
Preparation Time: 10 minutes
Total time: 30 minutes

Ingredients:

• Two - three pastured eggs, hard-boiled
• Pink Himalayan salt
• Half - 1 avocado
• One - two tbsp. of extra virgin olive oil
• Lemon juice
• One medium spring onion (15g/.five oz.)
• 1 small head crunchy lettuce

Instructions:

Boil the eggs.
In a bowl, put all the items and splash a little lemon juice.
Your salad is now ready to be enjoyed!

Nutrition Information:

Total calories: 279; Calories from fat: 225
Total fat: 25.5g; Saturated fat: 12.6g
Total carbohydrates: 9.1g; Fiber: 3.2g; Net carbohydrates: 5.9g
Protein: 8.6

Walnut Banana Bread

Servings: 12
Prep Time: 10 minutes
Cooking Time: 60 minutes

Ingredients:

- ¼ cup of oil
- 1 tablespoon of honey
- 1 tablespoon of vanilla essence
- 3 pasture-raised eggs
- 3 medium bananas
- 1 teaspoon of baking soda
- ¼ teaspoon salt
- 1 ½ cups of ground walnuts
- ¼ cup of coconut flour

Directions:

Preheat your oven to 350°F.
Grease an 8 x 4-inch loaf pan.
Blend the oil, honey, vanilla, eggs, and bananas in a food processor.
Blend in the other ingredients and pour into a prepared pan.
Bake for about an hour.
Leave it out to cool before turning out and slicing.

Nutrition Information:

Total calories: 596; Calories from fat: 351
Total fat: 39.7g; Saturated fat: 25.8g
Total carbohydrates: 11.9g; Fiber: 17.5g; Net
carbohydrates: 28.4g
Protein: 26.7g

Brilliant Berry Pudding Combo

Serves: 3
Preparation Time: 15 minutes
Total time: 40 minutes

Ingredients:

• One to two tablespoon of swerve, powdered or other healthy low-carb sweetener
• 1/2 cup of water or may be almond milk
• Five to nine drops of Stevia extract
• ¼ cup of coconut milk
• 1/2 cup of berries, either frozen or may be fresh
• ¼ cup of chia seeds, whole or ground
• Half tsp. of cinnamon

Instructions:

Blend in the stevia, swerve, or any low-carb sweetener, cinnamon, water, chia seeds, and coconut milk.
Then blend all items thoroughly until it becomes smooth.
Then, sprinkle it off with berries.
Now, you should keep it away and proceed to the succeeding step.
For about 10 to 15 minutes, let it settle, or maybe put it in the fridge, or let it stay overnight. It will be ready for your breakfast.
Just in case you want it to be smoother, you may combine all the items in a blender and then blend in the berries afterward.

Nutrition Information:

Total calories: 551; Calories from fat: 252
Total fat: 28.7g; Saturated fat: 23.7g
Total carbohydrates: 15.1g; Fiber: 5.2g; Net
carbohydrates: 9.9g
Protein: 17.3g

Lime Cheesecake

Serves: 3
Preparation Time: 20 minutes
Total time: 45 minutes

Ingredients:

- 8 ounces of softened cream cheese from grass-fed cows
- 1 tablespoon of vanilla
- ½ cup of organic grass-fed heavy whipping cream
- 6 packets of True Lime
- 3 whole pasture-raised eggs
- Artificial sweetener that is equal to 12 teaspoons of sugar

Instructions:

Beat the heavy cream and cream cheese using an electric mixer until it forms a smooth mixture.
Add the remaining ingredients and blend well.
Pour the batter into a ramekin, lined and greased, and put on a cookie sheet.
Insert a knife at the center of the mixture, then let it bake for 30 to 40 minutes at 350°F until the knife comes out clean.
Place on a rack until it cools and then refrigerate.
You can serve once cooled.

Nutrition Information:

Total calories: 320; Calories from fat: 288
Total fat: 32.2g; Saturated fat: 4.7g
Total carbohydrates: 26.8g; Fiber: 13.1g; Net
carbohydrates: 13.7g
Protein: 5.8g

Deviled Eggs

Serves: 2
Preparation Time: 5 minutes
Total time: 15 minutes

Ingredients:

- 6 large pasture-raised eggs
- ¼ teaspoon of French mustard
- 1 tablespoon of homemade mayonnaise
- A few drops of hot sauce (optional)
- 1 teaspoon of paprika
- 1 teaspoon of cumin (optional)
- 1/2 teaspoon of chili pepper
- Salt & pepper to taste
- Parsley to garnish

Instructions:

Remove the yolk from the hardboiled eggs.
Using a fork, mash the yolk and add the other ingredients.
Mix until everything blends in well to form a thick mixture.
Fill the eggs with the mixture and sprinkle paprika on the top.

Nutrition Information:

Total calories: 380; Calories from fat: 260

Total fat: 30.1g; Saturated fat: 8.5g
Total carbohydrates: 28.0g; Fiber: 20.1g; Net
carbohydrates: 8.9g
Protein: 19.4g

Coconut Macadamia Chia Pudding

Serves: 1
Total time: 5 minutes + overnight

Ingredients:

•3 tbsp. of chia seeds (Lectins)
•¼ cup of coconut cream
•¾ cup of water
•1 tbsp. of XCT oil
•Sweetener, optional
•2 tbsp. of raw macadamia nuts, chopped

Instructions:

Mix the first five ingredients and allow to sit for 8-12 hours, shaking occasionally if possible.
Serve with macadamia nuts.

Nutrition Information:

Total calories: 564; Calories from fat: 463
Total fat: 55.2g; Saturated fat: 35.2g
Total carbohydrates: 18.3g; Fiber: 13.1g; Net carbohydrates: 5.2g
Protein: 7.4g

Stuffed Mushrooms

Serves: 3
Preparation Time: 15 minutes
Total time: 50 minutes

Ingredients:

- 1 lb mushrooms
- ½ cup of chicken broth
- 8 ounces of Boursin cheese
- Paprika to garnish

Instructions:

Preheat the oven to 350 degrees F.
Remove the stems from the mushrooms, and reserve them for another use.
Fill all the mushrooms with Boursin, and place them in a baking pan.
Pour some chicken broth around the mushrooms to fill the bottom of the pan.
Spread lightly with paprika.
Bake for 30 to 40 minutes and serve hot.

Nutrition Information:

Total calories: 389; Calories from fat: 220
Total fat: 30.1g; Saturated fat: 9.5g

Total carbohydrates: 35.0g; Fiber: 19.1g; Net carbohydrates: 16.9g
Protein: 23.4g

Sweet and Tangy Creamy Pork

Serves: 2
Preparation Time: 10 minutes
Total time: 25 minutes

Ingredients:

- 2 tablespoons of canned jalapeno pepper slices (lectins)
- 1 teaspoon of coconut oil
- Liquid sucralose to taste
- ⅓ ounce of pork rinds
- ¼ cup of organic grass-fed whipped cream cheese

Instructions:

Mix the liquid sucralose with the peppers to get a hot, tangy, and sweet mixture.
Set aside while you melt the coconut oil over medium heat, and blend in with the whipped cream cheese.
Be careful not to use too many pork rinds or else you will mess the fat ratio; you can weigh them if you have a scale.
Spread the pork rinds with the cream cheese, add one slice of sweetened jalapeno, and serve.

Nutrition Information:

Total calories: 530; Calories from fat: 460
Total fat: 40.1g; Saturated fat: 6.5g

Total carbohydrates: 20.0g; Fiber: 10.1g; Net
carbohydrates: 10.9g
Protein: 15.4g

Jalapeno Poppers

Serves: 2
Preparation Time: 8 minutes
Total time: 20 minutes

Ingredients:

- 2 fresh jalapeno peppers (lectins)
- 2 slices of uncured pasture-raised bacon
- 1½ ounces of cream cheese

Instructions:

Prepare the peppers by splitting them and remove the stems and seeds.
Divide the cream cheese into two, and stuff each pepper.
Roll all the peppers in bacon and seal if you can (toothpicks are great to secure it).
Make sure to wash your hands thoroughly to remove any pepper left on your hands.
Broil or grill until the bacon is cooked.

Nutrition Information:

Total calories: 400; Calories from fat: 280
Total fat: 42.1g; Saturated fat: 4.5g
Total carbohydrates: 36.0g; Fiber: 20.1g; Net carbohydrates: 16.9g
Protein: 19.4g

Fettuccine with Pancetta Cream

Serves: 4
Preparation Time: 10 minutes
Total time: 25 minutes

Ingredients:

- 1 packet of fettuccini miracle noodles
- 1 tablespoon of grass-fed butter
- 1 ounce of pancetta (Italian bacon)
- 1 teaspoon of minced parsley
- ½ ounce of grass-fed cream cheese

Instructions:

Drain and rinse your noodles, and put them in a bowl.
Snip across them using your kitchen shears and then pan-fry them for two minutes, then cut the pancetta fairly fine.
Put a medium-sized skillet over medium-low heat, and let the bits to brown.
Stir in the pancetta.
Add the cream cheese and butter to the noodles, and let them melt to coat the noodles evenly.
Put the crispy pancetta bits and all the fat from the pan into the noodles.
Add the parsley, toss once more, and serve.

Nutrition Information:

Total calories: 345; Calories from fat: 312
Total fat: 30.1g; Saturated fat: 5.5g
Total carbohydrates: 45.0g; Fiber: 27.1g; Net
carbohydrates: 28.9g
Protein: 23.4g

Chocolate Almond Butter Bombs

Serves: 5
Preparation Time: 5 minutes
Total time: 15 minutes

Ingredients:

- 3 ounces of 85% dark chocolate
- 3 tablespoons of coconut oil
- 8 tablespoons of grass-fed butter
- 1 tablespoon of grass-fed heavy whipping cream
- 4 tablespoons of natural creamy almond butter
- ½ cup of raw macadamia nuts
- Sugar substitute equal to 6 teaspoons of sugar

Instructions:

Put the butter and chocolate on the stove to melt for a few seconds.
Add the rest of the ingredients, but leave the macadamia nuts and mix until smooth.
Stir in the macadamia nuts and pour about 2 to 3 teaspoons into each paper-baking cup.
Store in freezer.
Eat frozen or warm for 5 minutes.

Nutrition Information:

Total calories: 400; Calories from fat: 360

Total fat: 30.1g; Saturated fat: 8.5g
Total carbohydrates: 55.0g; Fiber: 33.1g; Net carbohydrates: 22.9g
Protein: 19.4g

Creamy Strawberry and Pecans

Serves: 2
Preparation Time: 10 minutes
Total time: 20 minutes

Ingredients:

- 1 tablespoon of chopped raw pecans
- French vanilla liquid stevia
- ⅓ cup of grass-fed sour cream
- 1 strawberry (In Season)

Instructions:

Sweeten the sour cream with the French vanilla liquid stevia in a small bowl (you can use a little vanilla extract if you don't want it too sweet).
Stir until uniformly sweetened.
Slice the strawberry.
Top with the strawberry and pecans, and serve.

Nutrition Information:

Total calories: 640; Calories from fat: 526
Total fat: 30.1g; Saturated fat: 8.5g
Total carbohydrates: 60.0g; Fiber: 33.1g; Net carbohydrates: 18.9g
Protein: 28.4g

Chicken Noodle Soup

Serves: 2
Preparation Time: 10 minutes
Total time: 30 minutes

Ingredients:

- 3 tablespoons of coconut oil
- 4 tablespoons of diced celery
- 2 tablespoons of chopped onion
- 2 cups of chicken broth
- 4 tablespoons of shredded carrot
- 1 package of miracle noodles
- 1 teaspoon of chicken bouillon concentrate

Instructions:

Melt the coconut oil in a medium saucepan over medium-low heat.
Add the vegetables and sauté for about five minutes.
Add the bouillon and chicken broth, then mix and bring to a simmer.
Reduce the heat, cover, and let it simmer for another 20 minutes until the veggies are soft.
While you wait for these to cook, then pan-fry your noodles for 2 minutes.
Add the noodles to the soup when the veggies are soft, then let it simmer for another minute and then serve.

Nutrition Information:

Total calories: 484; Calories from fat: 368
Total fat: 43.1g; Saturated fat: 7.8g
Total carbohydrates: 48.0g; Fiber: 26.1g; Net
carbohydrates: 12.9g
Protein: 27.4g

Asparagus with Wasabi Mayonnaise

Serves: 3
Preparation Time: 8 minutes
Total time: 20 minutes

Ingredients:

- ½ lb of asparagus
- ¼ teaspoon of wasabi powder
- 2 tablespoons of homemade mayonnaise
- 1 pinch of Splenda
- ¼ teaspoon of coconut aminos or soy sauce
- 1 tablespoon of coconut oil

Instructions:

Bake asparagus for 20 minutes at 400 degrees with coconut oil.
Mix the rest of the ingredients while stirring in a small dish.
When done, pour the mixture over the asparagus in a bowl and mix.
You can eat the cooked asparagus right away with the mayo, or you can refrigerate and eat it later.

Nutrition Information:

Total calories: 372; Calories from fat: 250

Total fat: 40.1g; Saturated fat: 4.5g
Total carbohydrates: 25.0g; Fiber: 19.1g; Net
carbohydrates: 8.9g
Protein: 29.4g

Pumpkin Pie

Serves: 1
Preparation Time: 10 minutes
Total time: 35 minutes

Ingredients:

- 15-ounce of 100% pure organic pumpkin puree
- 2 whole beaten pasture-raised eggs
- 4 ounces of softened goat cream cheese
- ½ cup of grass-fed heavy whipping cream
- ½ teaspoon of pumpkin pie spice
- 2 tablespoons of grass-fed whipped cream
- Artificial sweetener that is equal to ¼ cup of sugar

Instructions:

Preheat oven to 350°F.
Beat the cream cheese and pumpkin until they form a smooth mixture using an electric mixer.
Beat the eggs and add in the heavy cream, pumpkin pie spice, and sweetener.
Grease some ramekins, place them on a cookie sheet, and then pour the mixture.
Let this bake for one hour, or until a knife inserted in the middle comes out clean.
Let it cool and then serve, or put in refrigerator until you are ready to eat.

Nutrition Information:

Total calories: 388; Calories from fat: 320
Total fat: 30.1g; Saturated fat: 3.5g
Total carbohydrates: 15.0g; Fiber: 9.1g; Net
carbohydrates: 8.9g
Protein: 16.4g

Bonus#1: Homemade Mayonnaise

Ingredients:

- Pasture-raised egg yolk
- 3/4 cup of avocado oil
- 1½ teaspoons of fresh lemon juice
- ½ teaspoon of sea salt
- A teaspoon of white wine vinegar
- ¼ teaspoon of Dijon mustard

Preparation:

1. Mix the vinegar, egg yolk, mustard, lemon juice, and ½ teaspoon of salt into a bowl. Whisk till blended to bright yellow.
2. Use the ¼ teaspoon to measure to whisk constantly, put ¼ cup of oil into the yolk mixture, a drop at per minute, about 4 minutes.
3. Gradually put the remaining ½ cup of oil on a slow tiny stream, and whisk constantly, till thick, it will be much lighter color.
4. Lid to chill.

Bonus#2: The Loco Moco!

Ingredients:
- 1 pound of grass-fed ground beef
- 4 pasture-raised eggs
- Organic ketchup (lectin containing)
- 1 cup of basmati rice (From India)

Instructions:

Cook the rice first by adding one cup of rice and two cups of water and bring to a boil. As soon as it is boiling, turn the heat to low and let simmer for around 45 minutes.

Salt and pepper the beef and mix it around in a large bowl.

Form 4 round patties and cook them in butter in a medium-sized pan as desired.

Cook your 4 eggs sunny side up once the burgers are done in the same pan.

When the eggs are done, put the rice on the bottom of a huge bowl, place two burgers on top of the rice, then one egg on top of each burger. Cover in ketchup and ENJOY!

Calories – Do you even care?!?!?!?

Note From The Author

Thank you for reading the Ketogenic Cookbook!

If you enjoyed it, please consider posting an honest review on Amazon. Reviews are very important to us independent authors, and we appreciate every one we get. Stay tuned for my future healthy eating cookbooks coming soon on Amazon! If you would like to connect with me, please check out on my social media channels:

Facebook

Twitter

CPSIA information can be obtained
at www.ICGtesting.com
Printed in the USA
LVHW05s0008290618
582188LV00011B/1226/P